C000023254

LIVING STONES

BOULDERS

SUSAN SAYERS

Illustrated by
Fred Chevalier

Kevin
Mayhew

First published in 1999 by
KEVIN MAYHEW LTD
Buxhall
Stowmarket
Suffolk IP14 3BW

© 1999 Susan Sayers

The right of Susan Sayers to be identified as the author
of this work has been asserted by her in accordance
with the Copyright, Designs and Patents Act 1988.

All rights reserved. No part of this publication may be reproduced,
stored in a retrieval system, or transmitted, in any form or by any means,
electronic, mechanical, photocopying, recording or otherwise,
without the prior written permission of the publisher.

The contents of this book may be photocopied without copyright infringement,
provided they are used for the purpose for which they are intended.
Reproduction of any of the contents of this book for commercial purposes
is subject to the usual copyright restrictions.

0 1 2 3 4 5 6 7 8 9

ISBN 1 84003 399 1
Catalogue No 1500293

The other titles in the *Living Stones* series are

Complete Resource Book	ISBN 1 84003 396 7	Cat. No. 1500290
Prayers of Intercession	ISBN 1 84003 395 9	Cat. No. 1500294
Pebbles	ISBN 1 84003 397 5	Cat. No. 1500291
Rocks	ISBN 1 84003 398 3	Cat. No. 1500292

Cover photographs: Images Colour Library Limited, London
Cover design by Jaquetta Sergeant
Edited by Katherine Laidler
Typesetting by Kevin Whomes
Printed in Great Britain

FOREWORD

While many churches provide for the needs of the children, there is often an uncomfortable gap where young people are concerned. This is the age when deep questions are being asked, and it is essential that our young people find in their churches those who are going to listen and not be shocked; those who are willing to enter into real discussion and provide relevant and unsuffocating support during adolescence.

Many churches are well aware of the needs, but find it difficult to provide for them. They are concerned about this age group feeling too old for children's ministry but not able to relate to what adults are doing in church. Sadly, the result is often an exodus of young people, just when their faith could be (and often is) taking off.

Not only do our young people need the Church; the Church badly needs its young people. Their insistence on rejecting every hint of hypocrisy, and their gift of presenting challenging ideas with wit and enthusiasm – these are good for everyone and vital for a healthy body of Christ.

This programme aims to provide relevant and varied activities for young people which stimulate their thinking and encourage valuable discussion. Although some young people will be involved on the children's ministry team, I am convinced that they need feeding at their own level as well. Sometimes in their programme I have suggested that the young people put their ideas to the PCC. Do encourage the PCC to take such ideas seriously.

The factfiles on each week's worksheet can be collected into a book so that the course becomes a reference manual. It could also be used as an ongoing course for Confirmation or preparation for Communion.

The Boulders material provides a transitional course from separate ministry for children to full participation in the service with adults.

All the material in the book is copyright-free for non-commercial use.

SUSAN SAYERS

ACKNOWLEDGEMENTS

The publishers wish to express their gratitude to the following for permission to reproduce their copyright material in this publication:

CopyCare, PO Box 77, Hailsham, E. Sussex, BN27 3EF, for *Spirit of the Living God* (1963 Birdwing Music/Universal Songs), *I believe in Jesus* (chorus) (1987 Mercy/ Vineyard Publishing/Music Services), *Purify my heart* (chorus) (1990 Mercy/ Vineyard Publishing/Music Services), and *Jesus is Lord!* (verse 1) (1982 Springtide/ Word Music).

Darton, Longman & Todd Ltd, 1 Spencer Court, 140-142 Wandsworth High Street, London, SW18 4JJ, for the extract from *Audacity to Believe* by Sheila Cassidy, © 1992 Darton, Longman & Todd Ltd, and the extract from *A Glimpse of Glory* by Gonville ffrench-Beytagh, © 1986 Darton, Longman and Todd Ltd.

The Rt. Rev'd Timothy Dudley-Smith, 9 Ashlands, Ford, Salisbury, Wilts., SP4 6DY, for *Lord, for the years* (verse 5).

Hodder & Stoughton Ltd, 338 Euston Road, London, NW1 3BH, for the extract from *Child of the Covenant* by Michelle Guinness. Used by permission.

Iona Community, Pearce Institute, 840 Govan Road, Glasgow, G51 3UU, for *Jesus Christ is waiting* (verse 2). Taken from *Enemy of Apathy* (1988 Wild Goose Publications).

Kingsway's Thankyou Music, PO Box 75, Eastbourne, East Sussex, BN23 6NW, UK, for *Be still, for the presence of the Lord* (verse 3) (1986), *I'm accepted, I'm forgiven* (1985), *Meekness and majesty* (verse 2 and chorus) (1986) and *The King is among us* (verse 1) (1981). Used by permission.

Make Way Music, P.O. Box 263, Croydon, CR9 5AP, UK, for *Lord, the light of your love* (chorus). All rights reserved. International copyright secured. Used by permission.

OCP Publications, 5536 NE Hassalo, Portland, OR 97213, USA, for *Make me a channel of your peace* (dedicated to Mrs Francis Tracy) and *All that I am* by Sebastian Temple, (1967 OCP Publications). All rights reserved. Used by permission.

Josef Weinberger Ltd, 12-14 Mortimer Street, London, W1N 7RD, for *Lord Jesus Christ* (last verse) and *O Lord, all the world* (verse 4). Used by permission.

All other material contained in this publication is © Kevin Mayhew Ltd.

CONTENTS

ORDINARY TIME

RECOMMENDED BIBLES

It is often a good idea to look at a passage in several different versions before deciding which to use for a particular occasion, especially if you plan to involve several people in the reading.

For young people the New Century version of *The Youth Bible* includes various anecdotes and Bible studies which are inviting and challenging. A vivid version of the New Testament and parts of the Old Testament in contemporary language is Eugene Peterson's *The Message*. This catches the imagination and aids understanding. It is particularly good for reading aloud. *Into the Light* by the Bible Society is specially developed for reading aloud to those unused to the traditional language of the Church.

CHRISTMAS DAY AND MOTHERING SUNDAY

Christmas Day and Mothering Sunday are very much times for all God's children to worship together, and I have not included separate ideas or worksheets for the young people for these days.

Use some of the all-age suggestions in the *Living Stones* Complete Resource Book, or involve the young people in planning part of the service, and in the music group or choir, as servers, welcomers, collectors of the offering, decorating the church and so on.

ADVENT

First Sunday of Advent

Thought for the day

Be alert and watchful; keep yourselves ready.

Readings

Isaiah 64:1-9
Psalm 80:1-7, 17-19
1 Corinthians 1:3-9
Mark 13:24-37

Aim

To sense the longing for the Messiah and the need for rescue.

Starter

Try the short sketch about 'waiting' on page 125.

Teaching

Start by reading the passage from Isaiah, drawing out the way it moves in mood from 'If only' through 'But heck!' to 'Still, maybe?' Then look at 1 Corinthians 1. What has happened in the meantime to make for the hope and confidence expressed in Paul's letter? It is the life, death and resurrection of Jesus the Christ which has turned everything around.

Remind them that not only did Jesus come as our Saviour two thousand years ago; he is also going to come again, but this time in the full glory of God. Read the Gospel from Mark 13 and pick up on the clues and the unknowns, and the need to be watchful and ready.

Praying

O Lord, you are our Father.
We are the clay, you are the potter;
we are all the work of your hand.
Oh look upon us as we pray,
for we are all your people
in need of your mercy.

Activities

On the worksheet there is a bus queue of prophets with Bible references in their speech bubbles, so that the growing sense of need and longing for rescue is explored. There is also a selection of disaster pictures which link with the human condition spiritually and our need for rescue.

Discussion starters

1. Why does Jesus advise us to be alert and watchful?
2. How does the expectation of Jesus coming again with great power and glory affect the way we think and speak and act and spend in the meantime?

Notes

SECOND SUNDAY OF ADVENT

Thought for the day

John the Baptist prepares the way for the coming of the Messiah by helping the people to realign their lives.

Readings

Isaiah 40:1-11
Psalm 85:1-2, 8-13
2 Peter 3:8-15a
Mark 1:1-8

Aim

To look at Mark's treatment of John the Baptist's ministry, and the fulfilment of Isaiah's prophecy.

Starter

Have one of those frog toys with a suction pad which you press down and wait until it suddenly hops. (Or a rubber thimble for separating sheets of paper works just as well.) Take it in turns to start the thing off and everyone shouts, 'Now!' when they think it will pop up or hop.

Teaching

Read the beginning of Mark's Gospel, noticing how we are suddenly in the centre of all the action, and John seems to appear as if from nowhere. (Compare this with the first reference we get to the prophet Elijah's sudden appearance in 1 Kings 17:1.) Mark starts his account of Jesus with his public ministry, rather than the birth events, and John the Baptist is clearly the 'Elijah', the voice in the desert which the prophets had foretold.

Have a look at that prophecy in Isaiah 40, and look at how John was fulfilling it. See how the prophet is foretelling both the coming of Jesus in his ministry on earth and his second coming in all God's glory at the end of time.

Go back to the Gospel reading and discuss whether John seems to be calling individuals to repentance or the nation as a whole (or both). Why would baptism with water be a helpful symbol of what the people were doing spiritually?

Praying

Show us your unfailing love, O Lord,
and grant us your salvation.
I will listen to what God the Lord will say:
he promises peace to his people, his saints –
but let them not return to folly.
Surely his salvation is near those who fear him,
that his glory may dwell in our land.

(From Psalm 85)

Activities

There are various 'watery' experiences on the sheet to help pick up on the symbolism of water, and they are encouraged to look at different areas of their life which may need sorting out or cleaning up.

Discussion starters

1. Why is a repentant people more likely to be able to receive Jesus the Christ?

2. Forget, for a moment, the traditions of our Church, and imagine yourself on the shore of the river Jordan, having been totally immersed in cold water. In the light of this experience, how would you imagine being 'baptised with the Holy Spirit'? How did (and does) Jesus do this?

Notes

THIRD SUNDAY OF ADVENT

Thought for the day

In Jesus, God will be fulfilling the Messianic prophecies about the promised Saviour.

Readings

Isaiah 61:1-4, 8-11
Psalm 126 or Canticle: Magnificat
1 Thessalonians 5:16-24
John 1:6-8, 19-28

Aim

To see how the coming of the Messiah was God visiting and redeeming his people.

Starter

Each person in turn adds a word to a gradually developing sentence, so that some kind of story starts to take shape, which no one person has planned.

Teaching

All through the history of the people of Israel words were spoken by the prophets to reveal a bit more about what God meant and what God was like. Gradually the people started to grasp that one day God would be among his people to save them, in a new and very personal way. They started to think in terms of a Messiah, one anointed by God, who would come to them.

Look at the reading from Isaiah 61 to discover what the Messiah would be like. Pick out the characteristics in discussion and make a note of them. Then look at today's Gospel, stopping at verse 22. Why might they have thought that John was the Messiah or Elijah? (You can refer to the notes made.) Then read on to find out how John describes himself. Link this with the passage from Isaiah which you've just read. Why did John talk about the Messiah being already among them, though not yet known? (Think back to when John and Jesus had been born.)

Read through the Magnificat to see Mary praising God for what an amazing thing he has done. How does her excitement fit in with the Messiah promises, and the people's hopes?

Praying

With all my heart I praise the Lord
and I am glad because of God my Saviour.
He helps his servant Israel
and is always merciful to his people.
The Lord made this promise to our ancestors;
to Abraham and his family for ever.

(From the Magnificat)

Activities

On the sheet there is space to record some of the prophecies foretold about the Messiah, together with other references to look up which fill out the picture of a promised Saviour, given to the people of Israel through their history. They are also encouraged to look at what signs we should be expecting to see in a Christian church claiming to be followers of the way of the Messiah (or Christ).

Discussion starters

1. Why did the authorities want to check out John's identity and authority?

2. Examine the advice of the Thessalonians passage and look at how our lives, individually and as the Church, measure up.

Notes

FOURTH SUNDAY OF ADVENT

Thought for the day

God's promised kingdom, announced both to King David in ancient times and to Mary by the angel Gabriel, will go on for ever.

Readings

2 Samuel 7, 1-11, 16
Canticle: Magnificat or Psalm 89:1-4, 19-26
Romans 16:25-27
Luke 1:26-38

Aim

To see how the hope of a Messiah took shape through the years and was fulfilled in the birth of Jesus.

Starter

Provide crayons or heelball sticks to try some 'brass rubbing' on any effective surfaces (for example, coins, relief metal trays, shoe soles or manhole covers).

Teaching

Today we are looking at a gradually revealed picture of God's plan to save the world. Begin by reading the passage from 2 Samuel 7, noting the details of God's promise about the coming kingdom on a sheet of paper. Explain how, when the monarchy of Israel had crumbled, people started to think of this promised Saviour as a spiritual leader, rather than an ordinary worldly king. He became known as God's anointed, or chosen, One – the Messiah.

Then go on to read today's Gospel, with different people reading the parts of Mary and Gabriel. Go through the points noted already and tick those which match up. What about the coming king being of the house of David? (See verse 27.) Recap on King David's background (2 Samuel 7:8) and link his position with Mary's in Luke 1.46-55. Draw them to see how the ancient promise is being worked out through good people who make themselves available to God.

Praying

O come, O come, Emmanuel,
and ransom captive Israel,
that mourns in lonely exile here,
until the Son of God appear.
Rejoice, rejoice!
Emmanuel shall come to thee, O Israel.

Activities

On the sheet they can explore the nature of the Messiah, both as a priestly and a kingly figure, and there is the script of a conversation between two rocks on a hill near Bethlehem, remembering events there through the years and drawing attention to the historical and spiritual links of today's teaching.

Discussion starters

1. In the light of today's readings, why do you think Jesus put in so much teaching about the nature of the kingdom of God during his earthly ministry?

2. How can we further the kingdom and hasten its full coming?

Notes

1st Rock Gets cold when the sun's off your back, doesn't it?

2nd Rock Yeah – look, the lights are being lit down there in Bethlehem already.

1st Rock Do you remember that shepherd boy who used to sit on me and play his harp in the evenings?

2nd Rock How could I forget! King David, they made him in the end. What a fine young man he was!

1st Rock You know what I heard?

2nd Rock No – what?

1st Rock There's going to be another shepherd king born soon in Bethlehem – a descendant of our shepherd king, David.

2nd Rock A son of David! Isn't that the one who's supposed to reign over the whole world for ever?

1st Rock That's what they've been saying for the last thousand years.

2nd Rock I wonder if he'll come up here and sit on us?

1st Rock Mmm, that's a thought. Who knows – if we stick around here for another couple of thousand years...

2nd Rock ... which we will ...

1st Rock ... we might become famous, telling our story to other fine young men ...

2nd Rock ... and women ...

    1st Rock ... all over the world!

    Both What a thought!

ONE DAY A SON OF DAVID WILL REIGN

WHY WERE THE PEOPLE SO KEEN ON THEIR GREAT MESSIAH BEING FROM KING DAVID'S FAMILY?

Well, they looked back to David, the shepherd king, as the best king ever – a close friend of God, a good leader, and in touch with ordinary people.

SO THEY HOPED THE MESSIAH WOULD BE AS GOOD?

Better! They hoped God's chosen one would be like a perfect, priestly King David, who would reign for ever.

THAT SOUNDS LIKE JESUS, TO ME?

Yes, God's promise to David was repeated to Mary as she conceived Jesus!

? MESSIAH ?

O COME, O COME, EMMANUEL,
AND RANSOM CAPTIVE ISRAEL,
THAT MOURNS IN LONELY EXILE HERE,
UNTIL THE SON OF GOD APPEAR.
REJOICE, REJOICE!
EMMANUEL SHALL COME TO THEE,
    O ISRAEL.

EMMANUEL ~ 'GOD WITH US'

SHEPHERD OF HIS PEOPLE

KING

POWERFUL SAVIOUR

JUST AND RIGHTEOUS

SON OF KING DAVID

HOLY

HUMBLE

SON OF THE MOST HIGH

SAVING THROUGH SUFFERING

PRIEST

CHRISTMAS

FIRST SUNDAY OF CHRISTMAS

Thought for the day

Just as the angels said, a Saviour has been born for us.

Readings

Isaiah 61:10-62:3
Psalm 148
Galatians 4:4-7
Luke 2:15-21

Aim

To understand the right timing of Jesus' birth and the significance of the shepherds' visit.

Starter

Use the sketch on page 126.

Teaching

Begin by reading the passage from Galatians 4, which links up with the sketch in the starter. Then look at Isaiah, changing readers when you get to the new chapter so as to emphasise that from speaking as one of the people in Chapter 61 the prophet is now standing apart, pleading on behalf of the people – a link person between them and God.

Now explain how shepherds were considered 'unclean' outsiders because their job meant they were often in contact with dead bodies, and their working hours made it impossible for them to take a full part in the community's worship. Bearing this in mind, read the Gospel for today.

Praying

Praise the Lord from the heavens;
praise him all his angels.
Praise him, sun and moon;
praise him all you shining stars.
Praise the Lord from the earth,
you sea monsters and ocean depths;
fire and hail, snow and ice,
gales of wind that obey his voice.
Let kings and commoners, youths and girls,
old and young together,
let them praise the name of the Lord,
for his name is high above all others,
and his majesty above earth and heaven.

(From Psalm 148)

Activities

Using sounds and instruments this prayer can be expressed and recorded in music, or in artwork. Consider working on a large scale, using an old sheet, paints and large brushes or sponges. On the sheet the teaching about the shepherds is re-inforced with a shepherd's diary alongside some of the religious laws which they couldn't fail to break.

Discussion starters

1. Really good news alters lives. Share with the group any such news you remember receiving. Bearing in mind the religious standing of the shepherds, how might they feel on hearing the angels' news, and then on discovering the baby in the manger?

2. What factors can we see, with hindsight, which made this time 'right' for Jesus to be born?

Notes

GOOD TIMING

WHY WAS JESUS BORN WHEN HE WAS?

As far as God was concerned, this was the absolute best time for it to happen. Looking back we can see why.

HOW DO YOU MEAN?

Well, the people had learnt a lot about God through Egypt and their wandering in the desert, and in exile. They were as ready as they'd ever be.

THE ROMAN EMPIRE WOULD HELP THE GOOD NEWS SPREAD, TOO, WOULDN'T IT?

True. And Mary and Joseph were ready and willing to help.

– THE LAWS –

Anyone who eats anything found dead or torn by wild animals must wash his clothes and bathe and be ceremonially unclean till evening. Or else.

Anyone who picks up the carcass must wash his clothes and be unclean till evening.

Observe the Lord's Sabbath and do no work on it.

WHY WERE SHEPHERDS CONSIDERED 'UNCLEAN OUTSIDERS'??

SHEPHERD'S DIARY

Monday Found a lamb killed by a wolf. We cooked and ate it for tea. Washing will have to wait till we get to some water tomorrow, I'm afraid.

Tuesday Another lamb killed – by a rat. I killed the rat and dragged the carcass away from our sheep.

Sabbath Worked as usual, as the sheep were giving birth to their lambs, and they all needed feeding and protecting.

TRY TURNING THIS PRAYER INTO A PIECE OF MUSIC OR ARTWORK!

Ideas and Notes

PRAISE THE LORD FROM THE HEAVENS; PRAISE HIM ALL HIS ANGELS.
PRAISE HIM, SUN AND MOON; PRAISE HIM ALL YOU SHINING STARS.
PRAISE THE LORD FROM THE EARTH, YOU SEA MONSTERS AND
OCEAN DEPTHS;
FIRE AND HAIL, SNOW AND ICE, GALES OF WIND THAT OBEY
HIS VOICE.
LET KINGS AND COMMONERS, YOUTHS AND GIRLS, OLD AND
YOUNG TOGETHER,
LET THEM PRAISE THE NAME OF THE LORD,
FOR HIS NAME IS HIGH ABOVE ALL OTHERS,
AND HIS MAJESTY ABOVE EARTH AND HEAVEN.
(– FROM PSALM 148 –)

SECOND SUNDAY OF CHRISTMAS

Thought for the day

The Word made flesh at Christmas was always with God, always expressing his creative love.

Readings

Jeremiah 31:7-14 or Ecclesiasticus 24:1-12
Psalm 147:12-20 or Canticle: Wisdom of Solomon 10:15-21
Ephesians 1:3-14
John 1:(1-9) 10-18

Aim

To see how the Word can be seen present from the beginning.

Starter

Play hangman, where the word is there already and just needs them to uncover it.

Teaching

First read the Gospel for today, noticing the capital W in Word and discussing who John is talking about. In what way is Jesus God's Word? Was God's Word there at the beginning, as John says? (Look at Genesis to check.)

Now look at the Old Testament reading, picking up on the Word (sometimes thought of as the wisdom of God) being there all the time and not suddenly arriving on the hay in Bethlehem from nowhere. (Look at the picture on the sheet.)

Explain how John was writing for the Greek philosophers who would find it helpful to think of God in this way. Link it, too, with what God called himself when talking to Moses (Exodus 3:13-15) and with Jesus' 'I AM' teaching (John 8:58, for example).

Praying

Jesus, living Word of God,
you show us what loving means
and what it costs.

Activities

On the sheet they are encouraged to see God's Word in terms of the Trinity, and to explore the beginning of John's Gospel more deeply, expressing their ideas in drawing.

Discussion starters

1. Why do you think the eternal Word came into our world as a human baby, born as vulnerable and dependent as the rest of us?

2. How does our faith in Jesus affect the way we look at the books of the Old Testament?

Notes

THE WORD – GOD'S WORD

WHY DOES JOHN CALL JESUS THE WORD?

Well, what is someone's word?

I SUPPOSE IT EXPRESSES YOUR THOUGHTS.

Yes, that's right. And Jesus is the expression of God – he expresses God's love to us.

DID THAT START AT BETHLEHEM?

No. God spoke creation into being right at the beginning.

SO IN A WAY THE WORD OF GOD HAD ALWAYS BEEN THERE?

Yes.

TAKE THE BEGINNING OF JOHN'S GOSPEL (JOHN 1:1-18) AND TRY TO EXPRESS THE IDEA IN DRAWING.

THE WORD OF GOD

ALWAYS THERE	⇨	GENESIS 1:1-3
BORN	⇨	PSALM 147:15-19
LIFE STORY	⇨	JOHN 1:1-4

JESUS, LIVING WORD OF GOD,
YOU SHOW US
WHAT LOVING MEANS
AND WHAT IT COSTS.

EPIPHANY

THE EPIPHANY

Thought for the day

Jesus, the promised Messiah, is shown to the Gentile world.

Readings

Isaiah 60:1-6
Psalm 72:(1-9) 10-15
Ephesians 3:1-12
Matthew 2:1-12

Aim

To look at how people 'journey' to faith.

Starter

In a circle, pass a bus or train ticket around, and each person in turn says how they got here today. Then pass a cross around. Each person says how they're a Christian, or where they feel they are, how they got here and who has helped them on the way. (As with all circle time, those who don't wish to speak can pass the cross on, and it's fine to say the same as someone else has said if their situation is the same.)

Teaching

Start with today's Gospel reading, establishing what we know from the account about where they came from, how many and who they were. Draw attention to their not being Jewish, but pagan foreigners. Imagine together some of the dangers they may have faced on their journey. Why were they wanting to bother with it? How was the king they found different from what they were expecting?

Now look at Ephesians 3, reading verses 5-12, so they can see how Paul's calling was carrying on the mission to spread the good news to all the non-Jewish people, including us, if we are Gentiles. Finally look at Isaiah 60 to see how this had been prophesied generations before.

Praying

O Lord, our King,
let your kingdom come
in every nation
and every person,
starting with me.
Amen.

Activities

Make a banner or poster which expresses our many different journeys to Christ, who welcomes us wherever we have come from. On the sheet there are some examples of such journeys, and space to think about their own journey.

Discussion starters

1. Why do you think Matthew, writing for the Hebrew people, considered this event of the wise men's visit so important to include?

2. What can we, both as Gentiles and as members of the established Church, learn from the Magi visit about our own attitudes and calling?

Notes

ON A JOURNEY

WHY DID THE WISE MEN SET OUT TO FOLLOW A STAR?

Because they knew this star meant an important king had been born.

WHY WERE THEY INTERESTED IN A FOREIGN KING?

Because they had a hunch that this king would be king of the whole universe.

WHY DID THEY GIVE JESUS GOLD, FRANKINCENSE AND MYRRH?

Many people think they are symbolic presents – gold to show that Jesus is a king, frankincense for worship and myrrh for pain and suffering.

I came on the local Youth Bus and they were nice to me and told me about Jesus. Now I work on the Youth Bus too!

I felt there must be a God but I didn't know him. I asked lots of questions and people helped me to get to know him.

I was using drugs and my life was in a mess. A couple of Christian friends started praying for me and slowly I realised that God loves me.

I was brought up as a Christian and got to know Jesus when I was a child.

CHRIST

YOU!

JESUS WELCOMES US WHEREVER WE'VE COME FROM

EPHESIANS 3 : 4-12

O LORD, OUR KING, LET YOUR KINGDOM COME IN EVERY NATION AND EVERY PERSON, STARTING WITH ME.
– AMEN –

one man – ABRAHAM –

one family

one nation

one world!

Through the _ _ _ _ _ _ the _ _ _ _ _ _ _ _ _ are heirs together with _ _ _ _ _ _ , members together of _ _ _ body and _ _ _ _ _ _ _ together in the _ _ _ _ _ _ _ of Christ Jesus.

THE BAPTISM OF CHRIST: FIRST SUNDAY OF EPIPHANY

Thought for the day

Through the Holy Spirit, Jesus is affirmed at his Baptism as God's beloved Son, and we too are given the Spirit of God which affirms us as God's adopted daughters and sons.

Readings

Genesis 1:1-5
Psalm 29
Acts 19:1-7
Mark 1:4-11

Aim

To explore the presence of the Holy Spirit, particularly at Baptism.

Starter

Play the beginning of Haydn's Creation and give out paper and paints for them to express it in colour and form. As they paint, read the Genesis account above the music.

Teaching

Where is the Spirit of God in this passage? (Look at verse 2.) Point out that God cannot exist apart from his Spirit – the Holy Spirit is like the life, or breath, of God.

Now read Mark's account of Jesus' Baptism, noticing how the Spirit of God is portrayed here, and exploring why it might have seemed like a dove. Link this with the words God speaks to affirm Jesus in his identity and his mission.

Read Acts 19:1-7; in what ways is the Holy Spirit coming as at creation and at Jesus' Baptism? What are its effects? When they sense God's presence, is it like this or different again? Help them to see that God's Spirit comes to fill us only when we genuinely seek God and long to be filled with his life. How the Spirit comes varies, but always there is a sense of inner peace and joy, a deepening of love for God and a deepening realisation that God is real, alive and active.

Praying

Spirit of the living God, fall afresh on me!
Spirit of the living God, fall afresh on me!
Melt me, mould me, fill me, use me,
Spirit of the living God, fall afresh on me!

(Daniel Iverson
© 1963 Birdwing Music/Universal Songs/CopyCare)

Activities

The activities on the sheet help them to see how gentle, dynamic and creative the Holy Spirit is revealed to be in creation, in Baptism and in us.

Discussion starters

1. Why do you think Jesus was baptised by John when he didn't need to repent?

2. Is the thought of God's Spirit dwelling in us a little frightening; would we prefer God to keep his distance?

Notes

SECOND SUNDAY OF EPIPHANY

Thought for the day

Jesus, the Christ, unlocks the mysteries of God.

Readings

1 Samuel 3:1-10 (11-20)
Psalm 139:1-6, 13-18
Revelation 5:1-10
John 1:43-51

Aim

To know that we are called to follow the one who can 'show us the Father'.

Starter

One person tries to keep a completely still face, without responding to the others at all. They try their best to make the person laugh, but they can only use their voices (no tickling allowed).

Teaching

Sometimes we don't respond or answer when we're called, especially if we don't want to hear what we think someone is going to ask us! Other times, we're sitting waiting to be called and jump up to respond as soon as possible. Today we are going to look at people who are called and respond.

First read the passage from 1 Samuel, talking about the way Samuel heard God's call even before he realised it was possible for God to get in touch with him, and what he heard put him in the tricky position of having to give unpleasant and scary news to his guardian. God needed this young boy to do a particular job.

Now look at the reading from Revelation. There was only one person who could do this job of opening the hidden words of the scroll. Jesus was the only one who could do it.

Today's Gospel shows us Jesus calling some of his disciples from their ordinary lives to take part in the extraordinary work of accompanying the Son of God on his rescue mission of love. How do Philip and Nathanael respond? Philip immediately goes off to tell Nathanael about Jesus – he's bursting with the news. Nathanael is at first sceptical, but Jesus' knowledge of him convinces him that this person is worth cancelling everything for.

Jesus calls us for particular jobs of Christian living which only we can do.

Praying

Search me out, O God, and know my heart;
try me and know my restless thoughts.
Look well whether there be any wickedness in me
and lead me in the way that is everlasting.

(From Psalm 139)

Activities

On the worksheet there are some 'listening exercises', and tips for getting to know God better.

Discussion starters

1. Why do you think Jesus spoke of his ministry in terms of angels ascending and descending? (You may like to look at Genesis 28:12.)

2. If Jesus Christ is the one who reveals and makes clear the hiddenness of God, what does that suggest the Church should be doing – and are we doing it?

Notes

TUNING IN!

Slowly move the tuning knob so your friends hear tiny bits from each frequency . . .

1. Who can identify most radio stations?

   Name: **Number:**

2. Listen out specially for your local radio station and see who spots it first.

   Name:

BEING CALLED

DO PEOPLE HEAR GOD'S VOICE WHEN THEY'RE CALLED BY HIM?

Sometimes it sounds like a real voice – Samuel thought it was Eli calling him at first. But mostly God calls right into our being, so he doesn't need to vocalise it.

HOW DO YOU HEAR IT, THEN?

When God calls, you sense that he is communicating with you. It may be through the natural world, another person, something you see or read, or experience.

CAN YOU MISS HEARING GOD GETTING IN TOUCH WITH YOU?

Yes, if you try to block him out of your life.

IT'S ALL A QUESTION OF TUNING IN AND BEING READY TO HEAR!

TRY HEARING A MESSAGE WHILE YOU CRUNCH ON A RAW CARROT!

...CRUNCH, CRUNCH...

I ♥ CARROTS

Make time for God every day. If you don't feel like praying or don't know what to say, use ready-made prayers.

Tell God you're happy to be used in his work and then notice what happens

TIPS FOR GETTING TO KNOW GOD BETTER

When you mess things up, put it right with God straightaway. Let him forgive you and then enjoy making a fresh start.

As you try to treat people as Jesus would, you'll find that you are getting to know God better.

SEARCH ME OUT, O GOD,
AND KNOW MY HEART;
TRY ME AND KNOW MY RESTLESS THOUGHTS.
LOOK WELL WHETHER THERE BE
ANY WICKEDNESS IN ME
AND LEAD ME IN THE WAY
THAT IS EVERLASTING.
(-FROM PSALM 139-)

Third Sunday of Epiphany

Thought for the day

Signs of glory lead us to believe in Jesus as Lord and Saviour.

Readings

Genesis 14:17-20
Psalm 128
Revelation 19:6-10
John 2:1-11

Aim

To explore the meaning of the miracle at Cana in terms of a sign of glory.

Starter

Play 'Give us a clue', where signs are used to describe a film, book or TV programme title.

Teaching

Read the story of the wedding at Cana, with different people reading the various parts. Use the headings on the sheet to help explore the meaning of the story, establishing who was there, what each did, where it happened, and what it shows us about Jesus.

This leads on to the reading from Revelation, where the everlasting authority and worth of Jesus is affirmed. Read it together, looking out for the way it confirms what we have glimpsed in this first miracle of Jesus.

Praying

Manifest at Jordan's stream,
prophet, priest and King supreme,
and at Cana, wedding guest,
in the Godhead manifest,
manifest in power divine,
changing water into wine;
anthems be to thee addressed:
God in man made manifest.

DICTIONARY
manifest: shown to be, clear, revealed
anthems: songs of praise

Activities

On the sheet there are spaces to record the exploration of the Cana story and its meaning, and the normal route by which water becomes wine.

Discussion starters

1. If you had no church background, which events of the Gospels would lead you to consider worshipping Jesus as Lord?

2. Look at the different characters in the Cana wedding event and discuss what might have been going through their minds at each stage of the episode.

Notes

GUEST LIST

What happened?

THE WEDDING

AT CANA

MAP

SIGNS OF GLORY

DID JESUS LOOK ANY DIFFERENT FROM OTHER HUMAN BEINGS?

We don't have any description of his looks, but he looked quite normal.

SO HOW DID PEOPLE REALISE WHO HE WAS?

It was all to do with what he did; how he behaved and what he said.

WHAT ABOUT TURNING WATER INTO WINE, FOR INSTANCE?

Exactly. Signs like this marked Jesus out as being full of God's authority, and sharing God's glory.

WATER INTO WINE

SQUASH SQUASH...

④

⑤

①

②

③

⑥

JOHN 2:1-12 SHOWS US THAT... _____

What does it show us about JESUS?

MANIFEST AT JORDAN'S STREAM, PROPHET, PRIEST AND KING SUPREME, AND AT CANA, WEDDING GUEST, IN THE GODHEAD MANIFEST, MANIFEST IN POWER DIVINE, CHANGING WATER INTO WINE; ANTHEMS BE TO THEE ADDRESSED: GOD IN MAN MADE MANIFEST.

DICTIONARY

MANIFEST: Shown to be, clear, revealed

ANTHEMS: Songs of praise

FOURTH SUNDAY OF EPIPHANY

Thought for the day

Jesus displays all the signs that mark him out to be God's chosen One.

Readings

Deuteronomy 18:15-20
Psalm 111
Revelation 12:1-5a
Mark 1:21-28

Aim

To trace the prophecies through to the person of Jesus, displaying God's nature in his words and behaviour.

Starter

Play a card game in which you try to cheat, but if challenged you have to show whether you have been honest or not. One possibility is this. Deal out the cards equally. Players hide their hand of cards from everyone. Take it in turns to place cards face down in order of number, saying aloud what you are claiming it to be. If challenged, you must turn the card up, and if you are found to have cheated, you have to take all the cards laid on the table. First to be rid of all their cards wins.

Teaching

One of the top qualities of God is his complete integrity and honesty. God never pretends to us or cheats; his nature is full of truth. As people we often cheat, not just playfully in games but in our lives. We are quite good at doing wrong and pretending to ourselves that it is someone else's fault. If we don't like to think of ourselves as unkind, we'll sometimes pretend that we haven't been unkind, even though we secretly know we have.

That's why it has always been a bit unnerving when people have found God looking into their hearts, and realised that he sees what is really there, and not what we'd like him to find. His light shows up evil and wrong thinking as well as all the good stuff. Read the passage from Deuteronomy 18, noticing how the people even then were rather scared of close contact with the all-seeing God. Then go on to today's Gospel. In Jesus, God has come closer to his people than ever before, and there is a man in the congregation who finds this very distressing. Talk over why this might be, in view of what you read in the first reading.

Go back to the Deuteronomy passage and look at the verses about the prophet speaking God's word. Link this with Mark 1:22, so that they can pick up on the authority of Jesus as God's spokesman. Jesus is God's chosen One, and as he expresses God's thoughts and nature, people are bound to notice God's glory shining in him.

Praying

Lord Jesus, as we read about you in the Gospels
we can see that you are the Christ,
God's anointed, chosen Saviour.
We ask you to shine in us,
so that we are lit up by your truth and love.

Activities

On the sheet there is a role-play to try, and an identity markings activity which enables them to consider identity markings of the Messiah.

Discussion starters

1. What signs of glory showed in Jesus?

2. How can we get the right balance between awesome reverence which verges on fear, and familiarity which borders on presumption?

Notes

Elephant Hawk Moth
- 2 large eye spots behind the head
- front looks a bit like an elephant's trunk

Garden Tiger Moth
- covered with fuzzy hairs
- often known as a 'woolly bear'

Magpie Moth
- moves in a looping way, arching its back

Puss Moth
- uses its face mask and tail whips to display threateningly to its predators

"I KNOW WHO YOU ARE!"

THAT MAN SOUNDS REALLY FRIGHTENING, SCREAMING AT JESUS LIKE HE HATES HIM.

Yes, I expect it was quite scary to be there.

WHY DID HE THINK JESUS WAS GOING TO DESTROY HIM?

The evil spirit in him knew he was in the presence of God – enough to make any evil spirit panic.

JESUS SEEMS QUITE IN CONTROL, THOUGH.

That's because God's power of good is always stronger than the power of evil, and Jesus just wants to set the man free.

CAN YOU IDENTIFY THESE CATERPILLARS?

Peter, one of Jesus' followers, who was there in the synagogue (and had once said to Jesus, 'Go away from me, I'm a sinful man.')

Zeke, the man with an evil spirit, who has been sorted out by Jesus this morning

A visitor to Capernaum who hasn't heard what happened

WHAT IS IT THAT MARKS JESUS OUT AND IDENTIFIES HIM AS GOD'S CHOSEN ONE?

YOU ALL MEET UP ON THE SABBATH, AFTER GOING TO THE SYNAGOGUE IN CAPERNAUM.

Rebecca, who heard Jesus teaching before the healing, and was very impressed with his authority

LORD JESUS, AS WE READ ABOUT YOU IN THE GOSPELS WE CAN SEE THAT YOU ARE THE CHRIST, GOD'S ANOINTED, CHOSEN SAVIOUR. WE ASK YOU TO SHINE IN US, SO THAT WE ARE LIT UP BY YOUR TRUTH AND LOVE.

ORDINARY TIME

PROPER 1

Sunday between 3 and 9 February inclusive
(if earlier than the Second Sunday before Lent)

Thought for the day

The good news about God is far too good to keep to ourselves.

Readings

Isaiah 40:12-31
Psalm 147:1-11, 20c
1 Corinthians 9:16-23
Mark 1:29-39

Aim

To focus on what the good news is and how we can spread it.

Starter

Have a selection of newspaper headlines and stories. These are to be sorted into different categories:
• Gossip
• The odd/unusual
• Important good news
• Important bad news

Teaching

Leading on from the starter, talk together about what we consider is news worth spreading around in our newspapers each day. Notice which kind of stories are considered most newsworthy, and whether good news is considered worth printing. If they were to become an editor, would they want to change what is thought worth spreading?

Now read today's Gospel, looking at why Jesus wants to move on from Capernaum. What is it that he has seen in the eyes of those he has healed which makes him anxious to spread the good news as widely as possible? (Such things as joy and freedom from pain or guilt; they look as if they have just been set free.) The news we have to tell about Jesus is worth telling because lives can be set free as a result of knowing it. People surely have a right to know something that has the power to change their lives for the better.

Read the passage from 1 Corinthians to see how, for Paul, too, telling people about God's real power and presence is an urgent matter – he can't bear for anyone to be left without the opportunity to know God and benefit from his saving love.

Finally go back to the reading from Isaiah, to look at how the great God is described by the prophet, who also is doing his best to introduce people and help them realise how wonderful God is.

Praying

O God,
let no one miss out on knowing you
because I failed to let them know about you.
But rather let many be brought to love you
because of my words and actions.

Activities

On the sheet they are encouraged to think through the value of telling people certain information, both good and bad, and the responsibility of those who are in the know to inform other people of risks and benefits. They can then discuss what they want people to know about God, and how this might best be communicated to those who don't know God at all.

Discussion starters

1. What would you most want people to know about God?

2. What do you think is the best way of telling them?

Notes

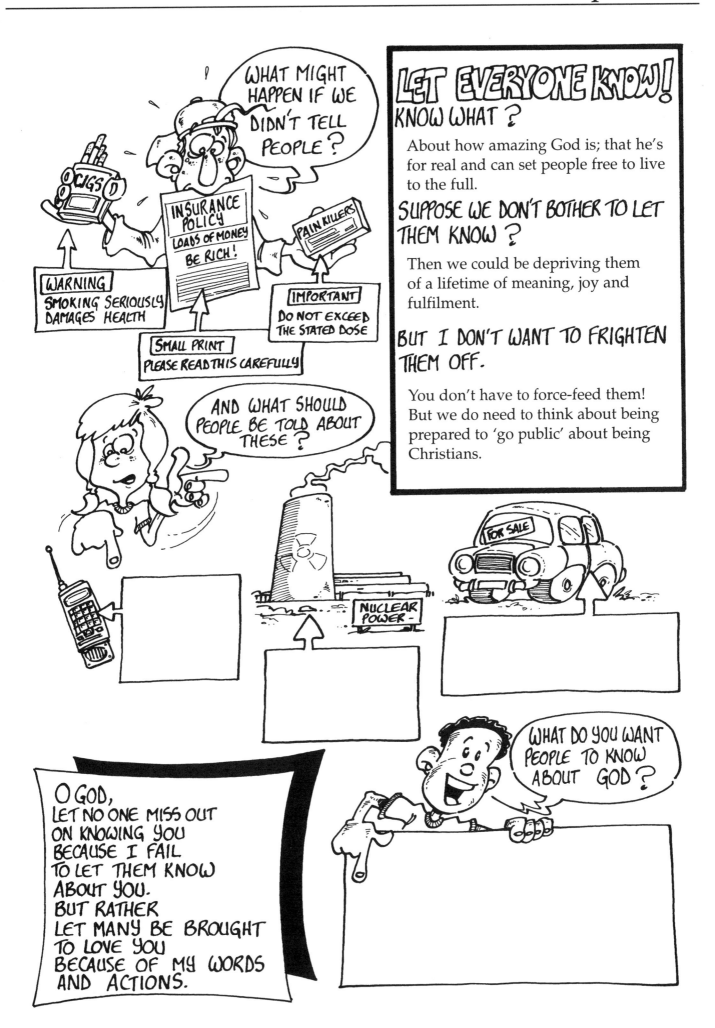

PROPER 2

Sunday between 10 and 16 February inclusive
(if earlier than the Second Sunday before Lent)

Thought for the day

Jesus wants to heal us to wholeness, and to him no one is untouchable.

Readings

2 Kings 5:1-14
Psalm 30
1 Corinthians 9:24-27
Mark 1:40-45

Aim

To see how God feels about untouchables.

Starter

On separate pieces of card, write out the following: a tramp; a mother with a noisy baby; a white man; a black man; a person with flu; a person with leprosy; a tattooed skinhead; a pretty girl; a handsome young man; an old lady who smells; a smoker; a disabled person; someone from a rival school.

Spread these cards out and let the group suggest a rating of 1-10 for their response to this question in each case: 'Would you be happy sitting on a crowded bus next to . . . ?'

Teaching

In the previous activity we could see that most of us have hang-ups about close contact with people in certain situations, for all kinds of reasons. It's easy to see why society clubs together to isolate certain groups, treating them as outsiders. Our readings today help us to see what God's attitude is to social outcasts and 'untouchables'.

Begin by reading the Gospel from Mark 1. Point out that in law this man was ritually unclean, and anyone touching him would be considered contaminated, and therefore unclean themselves. What was Jesus showing by touching the leper as part of the healing? Was it just the leprosy he was healing, or would the man have also been emotionally healed in some way by the touch?

Jesus' great desire to help the man to wholeness obviously overcame any thoughts of contamination; he reckoned it worth being 'contaminated', worth being thought 'unclean'. How does that link up with the idea of the Incarnation – 'Word of the Father, now in flesh appearing'? What does it all tell us about God and his attitude to us?

Now look at the passage from Corinthians, where Paul advises us all to check our own behaviour seriously. In view of today's Gospel, how do we measure up? Do we reach out to touch, or do we go along with what everyone else considers OK to ignore and avoid?

Praying

Lord God, make me willing
to reach out with your love
and touch the lives
and look into the eyes
of those whom the world despises and avoids.
Amen.

Activities

On the sheet there are examples of people working with the rejected and considering it a privilege as well as a responsibility. You could add to these with other examples, or invite someone in the parish who is working in such an area to join the group. There is also a thinking exercise to face the uncomfortable 'reasons' we have for rejecting and marginalising people. This week's teaching could well lead the group on to think of ways they can get more actively involved with local projects.

Discussion starters

1. Are there habits of social behaviour we have become so used to that we fail to see in them the marginalisation and degrading which is going on?

2. Do we ignore injustice when to act or speak out might make us unpopular? As Christians, what can we do about this?

Notes

IF YOU WANT TO, YOU CAN ...

SO THE LEPER BELIEVED THAT JESUS WAS ABLE TO CURE HIM?

Yes, he believed in Jesus' power, but he wasn't sure Jesus would want to do it.

THAT WAS A BIT OF AN INSULT, WASN'T IT? I MEAN, OF COURSE JESUS WOULD WANT TO HEAL HIM!

Exactly. But Jesus picks up on the way the man seems to think he's rubbish, and shows him that he isn't.

HOW?

By touching him! (He's supposed to be untouchable, remember.) And the man is healed.

*(Speech bubbles in illustration:)*

YES, IT'S THE CALCUTTA HOME FOR THE DESTITUTE AND DYING, BUT IT'S A HAPPY PLACE, FULL OF PEACE AND QUIET JOY. IT'S A GREAT PRIVILEGE TO BE HERE!

WE PROVIDE A HOT MEAL AND SHELTER FOR THE NIGHT.

IT'S NOT MUCH, BUT IT'S THE LEAST WE CAN DO, ISN'T IT?

WHAT DO YOU THINK MAKES SOMEONE THINK OF ANOTHER HUMAN BEING AS UNTOUCHABLE?

LORD GOD, MAKE ME WILLING TO REACH OUT WITH YOUR LOVE AND TOUCH THE LIVES OF THOSE WHOM THE WORLD DESPISES AND AVOIDS —
—AMEN—

They are 'different'	
They are offensive to look at	
They are offensive to listen to	
They are too poor	
They are too rich	
They threaten your own health	
They are embarrassing	
They are too demanding	

BUT ARE THESE **VALID** REASONS???

PROPER 3

Sunday between 17 and 23 February inclusive
(if earlier than the Second Sunday before Lent)

Thought for the day

The Son of Man has authority on earth to forgive sins.

Readings

Isaiah 43:18-25
Psalm 41
2 Corinthians 1:18-22
Mark 2:1-12

Aim

To explore the nature of God's forgiveness and Jesus' claims of identity.

Starter

Who am I? They have twenty questions in which to discover the identity of a chosen character. All questions can only be answered with a 'Yes' or 'No'.

Teaching

First read the Gospel together, with different people taking the parts and everyone reading the crowd's words. Look at what the scribes are thinking and wondering about. Why do they say, 'Only God can forgive sins'? Refer to the passage from Isaiah 43, seeing what God, through the prophet, has to say. Draw out that it is all part of God's loving goodness to forgive sins – his very nature is to do it. Look at what forgiveness actually means, using the sheet to focus your ideas, and then refer to 2 Corinthians 1:18-21. How does the Gospel show in action in verses 19 and 20? In Jesus forgiving the man's sins and healing him, he is acting out God's nature. So did he have the authority to forgive sins? Yes, because he was showing that he must indeed be the Son of God.

Praying

I'm accepted, I'm forgiven,
I am fathered by the true and living God.
I'm accepted, no condemnation,
I am loved by the true and living God.
There's no guilt or fear as I draw near
to the Saviour and Creator of the world.
There is joy and peace as I release
my worship to you, O Lord.

(Rob Hayward © 1985 Kingsway's Thankyou Music)

Activities

On the sheet they are encouraged to look at what forgiveness is, when we need it and how it can change our lives. It is important that they realise Christians are not perfect just because they go to church, and the Church is full of redeemed sinners. They also need to know that the forgiveness is not a once-off event, after which we lose the chance of God forgiving us again. There is *always* the opportunity to confess our sin to God and know his healing forgiveness.

Discussion starters

1. How can forgiveness be a healing?

2. In what way is Christ the eternal 'Yes'?

Notes

WHEN DO WE NEED GOD'S FORGIVENESS ???

"YOUR SINS ARE FORGIVEN"
DOES GOD MEAN HE'S DECIDED TO OVERLOOK OUR SINS?

No. He means that through his power of good over evil they are melted away completely, drowned in his love.

WOW! ONLY GOD COULD DO THAT.

Yes, that's right. We can forgive each other in the sense of 'dropping the charges' and coming to a loving agreement, but even then it's God's forgiveness we're tapping into.

SO GOD CAN GIVE US A COMPLETELY FRESH START, THEN?

He certainly can.

HOW IS FORGIVENESS LIKE SURGERY?

3 CHRISTIANS WHO KNOW GOD HAS FORGIVEN THEM!

LOOKED DOWN ON EVERYONE

GOD'S FORGIVENESS HAS CHANGED MY WHOLE LIFE!

FORMERLY IN PRISON FOR ATTEMPTED MURDER

ONLY LIVED TO MAKE MONEY AND SPEND IT ON HERSELF

I'M ACCEPTED, I'M FORGIVEN,
I AM FATHERED BY THE TRUE AND LIVING GOD.
I'M ACCEPTED, NO CONDEMNATION,
I AM LOVED BY THE TRUE AND LIVING GOD.
THERE'S NO GUILT OR FEAR AS I DRAW NEAR
TO THE SAVIOUR AND CREATOR OF THE WORLD.
THERE IS JOY AND PEACE AS I RELEASE
MY WORSHIP TO YOU, O LORD.

(Rob Hayward
© 1985 Kingsway's Thankyou Music)

SECOND SUNDAY BEFORE LENT

Thought for the day

Christ is the image of the unseen God.

Readings

Proverbs 8:1, 22-31
Psalm 104:24-35
Colossians 1:15-20
John 1:1-14

Aim

To explore the nature of God's creative wisdom.

Starter

Have an assortment of minerals, plants and shells for them to identify, using suitable reference books.

Teaching

Read the first four verses from John 1, with the objects they have been identifying spread out on calendar pictures of the world's beauty, while you read. Look at how complex and organised, varied and extraordinary that creation is. The objects and pictures are just a very few examples of it all.

John is saying that the person we know as Jesus Christ, although he became flesh at that point in time, had always been there, right from the beginning – in fact, just as his earthly life expresses God, so at the creation it was this 'expressive Word' with which God spoke the universe into being.

Now look at the reading from Colossians. Paul is quoting an early hymn, which is thinking over the same idea that we've just read in the introduction to John's Gospel. Check the similarities together.

We can go around most of the time with our heads down, occupied with all the everyday things like eating, socialising and spending money, but sometimes it suddenly occurs to us to ask ourselves what we're here for, and how we come to be whizzing round on this particular chunk of solidified gases in the universe. If we start looking and listening to what is all around us, we notice the distinctive mark of the God who created it; the mark of a wise and all-powerful Being, full of love.

Praying

Christ is exactly like God
who cannot be seen.
He is the firstborn Son,
superior to all creation.
God himself was pleased
to live fully in his Son.

Activities

On the sheet there are various words which make things happen. This leads them on to look at the power of God's creative Word. There is also a short cartoon script to start discussion about the basic question of the meaning of life. It is important that young people feel able to discuss all their questions and doubts; these should be seen as a vital part of faith development.

Discussion starters

1. If we who believe have the right to become 'children of God' by adoption, how would you expect our redeemed lives to look?

2. God created people in his own image as both male and female; Wisdom and the Spirit are both referred to as 'she', and the Word of God became flesh as a male. What do we miss if our understanding of God is predominantly 'male'?

Notes

ALL THINGS WERE MADE THROUGH HIM

IT'S A PRETTY IMPRESSIVE UNIVERSE, BUT WE'RE ONLY PARTS OF IT, SO HOW COME WE CAN THINK TO ASK HOW IT HAPPENED AND WHO MADE IT?

God made us a little bit like he is – and all around we've got proof that he thinks pretty impressive thoughts! So we are made able to think and wonder.

COULD IT ALL JUST BE RANDOM CHANCE, THOUGH? LIKE AN ACCIDENT?

Look closely. It doesn't look much like an accident! And there's another thing.

WHAT'S THAT?

We don't just see God expressed in this universe – we see him in person as well.

YOU MEAN JESUS?

That's right. God breaking into his own creation. That's love for you.

SUNDAY BEFORE LENT

Thought for the day

God's glory shows.

Readings

2 Kings 2:1-12
Psalm 50:1-6
2 Corinthians 4:3-6
Mark 9:2-9

Aim

To see that Jesus is glorified both on the mountain and on the cross.

Starter

Beforehand prepare a message which they can communally discover by making a rubbing of it. (Cut out each letter of the message from cardboard and stick the letters on a card or paper base. Cover the whole thing with lining paper, secured with sticky tape.) Give everyone wax crayons to rub over the lining paper in order to see the message:

NOW YOU HAVE SEEN
THE HIDDEN MESSAGE!

Teaching

Point out that the message was just as much there before they saw it; it was simply hidden from view. Today we are going to look at a time when God's glory became very obvious in Jesus. Read Mark's account of the Transfiguration on the mountain top. Think over what it revealed about Jesus, what it made clear and plain. (That Jesus was God's Son; he was filled with God's glory; he had God's authority; he was fulfilling the Law and the prophets; suffering and death had to be part of the rescue plan.)

How else in his life did Jesus show God's glory, but not by literally 'shining' with it? (In the way he spoke and taught; the way he healed and comforted; and, above all, in being willing to die a cursed death on the cross.)

Look at what John says about this in his Gospel (John 1:14).

Also read the Psalm for today, verse 3, and Exodus 3:2, Exodus 13:21, Deuteronomy 4:24, 2 Kings 2:11 and Daniel 7:9-10. Notice how the image of shining brightness and fire is seen as a sign of God's presence.

Praying

Shine, Jesus, shine,
fill this land with the Father's glory;
blaze, Spirit, blaze,
set our hearts on fire!

(From the song by Graham Kendrick
© 1987 Make Way Music)

Activities

There is space on the sheet to explore the references in more detail, and look at the crucifixion in terms of 'the Son of Man being glorified'. They can also try expressing this shining glory in a collage of words suggested on the sheet, using glowing, shining paper and foil. Have a variety of materials available.

Discussion starters

1. Are we wary of God showing his glory, preferring to 'tone him down'?

2. How do you think the transfiguration helped the disciples who witnessed it?

Notes

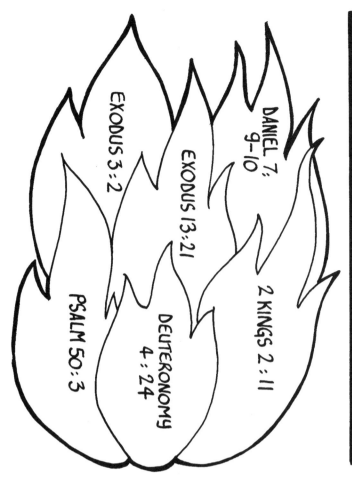

EXODUS 3:2

EXODUS 13:21

DANIEL 7:9-10

PSALM 50:3

DEUTERONOMY 4:24

2 KINGS 2:11

ON THE MOUNTAIN

IS THERE ANY REASON WHY IT HAPPENED ON A MOUNTAIN?

Well, mountains were thought of as holy places.

BECAUSE THEY'RE HIGH, AND SET APART FROM ORDINARY LIFE?

Yes, that's right. And traditionally God had shown his glory on mountains.

DIDN'T MOSES GET THE TEN COMMANDMENTS ON A MOUNTAIN?

He did indeed.

WHY WAS JESUS SEEN TALKING WITH MOSES AND ELIJAH?

Moses represented God's Law and Elijah God's prophets. So Jesus was seen to be Messiah, fulfilling the Law and the prophets.

WRITE THE KEY WORDS AND PHRASES AROUND THE FLAMES IN THE GLORY OF GOD - USE COLOURS OF FLAME AND SHINY PAPER TO CREATE A COLLAGE OF GOD'S GLORY!

HOW COULD THIS BE CALLED GLORY?

SHINE, JESUS, SHINE,
FILL THIS LAND WITH THE FATHER'S GLORY;
BLAZE, SPIRIT, BLAZE,
SET OUR HEARTS ON FIRE!

(From the song by Graham Kendrick
© 1987 Make Way Music)

CLUES
• GOD'S GLORY IS LOVE, SHINING
• WHAT DOES THE CROSS SAY ABOUT LOVE?
• HOW CAN GOD'S GLORY SHINE IN OUR WORLD?

LENT

First Sunday of Lent

Thought for the day

After his Baptism Jesus is led by the Spirit into the wilderness before returning to proclaim God's kingdom.

Readings

Genesis 9:8-17
Psalm 25:1-10
1 Peter 3:18-22
Mark 1:9-15

Aim

To look at the value of Jesus' time in the desert and our season of Lent.

Starter

Set up a short orienteering course, with something to collect from each point as they reach it. You will need to make a chart of the area on squared paper, marking the squares with numbers and letters (as shown below) so that they can find their way by map co-ordinates.

Teaching

Going through life is rather like finding our way through a landscape, and we need maps and a compass to guide us. Jesus referred to himself as the Way, which we can follow and trust. But, before he was able to start on that ministry, he had some working out to do himself.

Read the Gospel for today. What happened straight after Jesus had been baptised? Did he start his work immediately? No, he went out into the loneliness and discipline of the desert for forty days to search out what his role was, and how he needed to be spending the rest of his life on earth. It was a time of severe and difficult testing, which he had to go through, keeping to the right direction by keeping close to God and his word in scripture, as the doubts and temptations battled in him.

Only then could he come back into circulation and start his life's work. What are we told his work was? Proclaiming that God's kingdom is very near.

Now look at Noah and his family, setting out into the new, post-flood world. What do they receive from God to set them up for the rebuilding work ahead? God's promise of faithful, sustaining love, in the sign of the rainbow.

Lent gives us a chance to spend the same amount of time as Jesus spent in the desert, facing ourselves and our commitment to living God's way; to live more simply and rigorously while we allow God to prepare us for our own ministry as baptised Christians, proclaiming the risen Christ. It's all carefully thought out that Easter, the festival celebrating Christ's Resurrection, follows straight on from this 'desert season' of Lent.

Praying

Lead us, heavenly Father, lead us
o'er the world's tempestuous sea;
guard us, guide us, keep us, feed us,
for we have no help but thee;
yet possessing every blessing
if our God our Father be.

Activities

On the sheet there are some desert questions to reflect on, and some more teaching about Lent, with suggestions for using it profitably. Encourage the young people to take part in the parish Lent course, or lay one on specifically for them.

Discussion starters

1. Why can God only work with us in earnest when we are totally honest with him?

2. What is it that makes us decide whether or not discipleship is too costly?

Notes

Read through the whole of Mark's Gospel (that's less than 3 chapters a week).

If your church has a Lent course, join in. (If it hasn't, show this and ask for a suitable one!)

Live your life a bit more simply – spend less, for instance.

Write in a DAILY prayer time on your schedule and stick to it.

1. The church colour for Lent is

green	
purple	
red	

2. Jesus was in the desert for

42	
7	
40	

days

3. Christians use Lent to prepare themselves for the festival of

Easter	
Christmas	
Pentecost	

4. Lent is a time for fasting and prayer. Fasting means

practising self-control by going without food	
practising for a race by going fast	
practising prayer by speaking quickly	

SECOND SUNDAY OF LENT

Thought for the day

A commitment of faith has far-reaching implications.

Readings

Genesis 17:1-7, 15-16
Psalm 22:23-31
Romans 4:13-25
Mark 8:31-38

Aim

To explore the implications of placing our faith in God.

Starter

Blindfold everyone securely and lead them in a line through doorways and up stairs, quietly giving guidance to the one immediately next to you, so they all start warning one another of hazards approaching, and are therefore developing group trust.

Teaching

The blindfolds make us all more vulnerable, so we have to start looking after one another and our trust in one another grows. Sometimes we go through dark times in life, but we can trust God right through them. Read the passage from Genesis to see how Abraham was willing to go on trusting in God, even when there didn't seem to be much chance of God's promise coming true. Then read Romans 4, where Paul sees all those who stick with God in faith as being the real descendants of Abraham, including the Gentiles – including us!

Jesus wanted to prepare his disciples for a very dark time ahead, when he knew their faith would be shaken. It is quite typical of God to prepare us before some severe time of testing. Read the Gospel to find out how Jesus honestly and openly tells his followers what to expect, and still promises that if they stay firm, all will be well.

Praying

I believe in you, Lord;
I believe you are the Son of God.
I believe you died and rose again;
I believe you paid for us all.

(Taken from the song *I believe in Jesus* by Marc Nelson
© 1987 Mercy/Vineyard Publishing/Music Services/CopyCare)

Activities

On the sheet they are encouraged to think through Abraham's faith, and also their own commitment to follow Jesus, whatever the cost.

Discussion starters

1. In what sense are we descendants of Abraham?

2. Why is it that living God's way of love inevitably leads us into conflict?

Notes

HAVING FAITH

WHY DID ABRAHAM GO ON BELIEVING GOD'S PROMISE, EVEN WHEN HE AND SARAH WERE TOO OLD TO HAVE CHILDREN?

Because he knew God would keep his word – even though he couldn't see how.

IT MUST HAVE BEEN HARD TO GO ON BELIEVING IN JESUS AS A SAVIOUR WHEN THE ROMANS WERE HAMMERING NAILS INTO HIM. Yes, it must have looked like a complete flop. Many felt God had let them down that day.

BUT JESUS HAD TRIED TO WARN THEM ABOUT HIS DEATH, HADN'T HE?

Oh yes, but we often find it hard to believe what we don't want to hear.

THE RESURRECTION WAS A PRETTY DRAMATIC TURN-AROUND, WASN'T IT?

Well, there you are – God DOES keep his word!

I AM NEARLY 100!

I'D NEED A SON AND I HAVEN'T GOT ONE

SARAH'S TOO OLD TO HAVE CHILDREN NOW

HOW CAN I POSSIBLY BE THE FATHER OF A WHOLE NATION!

THERE WERE PLENTY OF GOOD REASONS FOR ABRAHAM TO GIVE UP ON GOD'S PROMISE...

BUT I KNOW GOD ALWAYS KEEPS HIS WORD!

BUT ONE GOOD REASON FOR HIM TO KEEP FAITH WITH GOD

WHAT DO WE GAIN IF WE HAVE THE COURAGE TO TAKE UP THE CHALLENGE OF THE CROSS?

WHAT STOPS US FROM TAKING UP OUR CROSS AND FOLLOWING JESUS?

I BELIEVE IN YOU, LORD;
I BELIEVE YOU ARE THE SON OF GOD.
I BELIEVE YOU DIED AND ROSE AGAIN;
I BELIEVE YOU PAID FOR US ALL.

(Taken from the song *I believe in Jesus* by Marc Nelson
© 1987 Mercy/Vineyard Publishing/Music Services/Copycare)

THIRD SUNDAY OF LENT

Thought for the day

God's wisdom may shock us. Jesus, obedient to God's Law and fulfilling it, dies a death which, according to the Law, makes him cursed.

Readings

Exodus 20:1-17
Psalm 19
1 Corinthians 1:18-25
John 2:13-22

Aim

To explore the implications of obeying God's Law.

Starter

They invent a simple ball game with clear rules, which gives everyone a chance to be involved.

Teaching

Point out the value of the rules, which make it possible for the game to be played and uphold fair play. Before you read the ten commandments from Exodus, check that they remember who is being given these rules and when. (The people of Israel, through their leader, Moses, after they had escaped from slavery in Egypt and were wandering in the wilderness.)

As each of the commandments is read (reading around the group), place cards of individual commandments on the table, together with memory joggers as follows: a large number one; a blank piece of paper; a cardboard speech bubble with 'Keep it Clean' written on it; a calendar page with Sunday circled in red; a bunch of flowers with a label reading 'To Mum and Dad'; a gun; a wedding congratulations card; a swag bag; a file clearly labelled 'Lies'; and a thought bubble with 'If only . . .' written on it.

Draw attention to the first commandment, and discuss what they might expect God's temple to be like, in the light of this rule. You could also refer to Isaiah 56:7. Bearing those ideas in mind, read the Gospel for today, so they can see how far the people had wandered from God's will as expressed in that first commandment.

How was Jesus being obedient to God's Law? When might obedience to God mean getting into trouble with the Law?

Praying

Jesus Christ is raging, raging in the streets
where injustice spirals and all hope retreats.
Listen, Lord Jesus, I am angry too;
in the kingdom's causes let me rage with you.

(Taken from the song *Jesus Christ is waiting*
by John L. Bell and Graham Maule
© 1988 WGRG, Iona Community)

Activities

On the sheet there is an obedience quiz and some headline situations to get them thinking about what makes them angry 'in the kingdom's causes', and what might be done about such things. The discussion may lead on to wanting active involvement in working for justice, peace and reconciliation. Useful resources for this are:

- Amnesty International – 99-119 Roseberry Avenue, London EC1R 4RE
- CARE – 53 Romney Street, London SW1P 3RF
- Christian Aid – PO Box 100, London SE1 7RT
- Christians Aware – 2 Saxby Street, Leicester LE2 0ND
- Evangelical Alliance – Whitefield House, 186 Kennington Park Road, London SE11 4BT
- Tearfund – 100 Church Road, Teddington TW11 8QE

Discussion starters

1. In what way is the 'Law of the Lord' refreshing to us, reviving the spirit?

2. What was it about the temple that made Jesus so angry? Might he find anything in our churches to anger him?

Notes

MORE DESERT QUESTIONS

OBEDIENCE QUIZ

1. You see someone struggling to get a baby stroller down a flight of steps you're walking up. Do you give them a hand?

2. You know that as a Christian you should be reading the Bible regularly. Are you making an effort to do it?

3. 'Forgive our trespasses *as we forgive.'* Any outstanding forgiving to be done?

4. Is it ever OK to lie?

... TO MEASURE BY ...

LOVE GOD : LOVE ONE ANOTHER

5. Are you spending some time each day praying?

GETTING ANGRY

WE DON'T OFTEN SEE JESUS AS ANGRY AS THIS, DO WE?

No – you can really feel him seething as he upsets all those tables, can't you?

ISN'T IT WRONG TO BE ANGRY LIKE THAT?

Losing your temper and lashing out is wrong, but we're meant to get angry at things which are very wrong – then we're inspired to put them right.

MARKETS AREN'T WRONG THOUGH, ARE THEY?

Oh no! What Jesus was angry about was turning God's house into a market, when it was meant to be a house of prayer.

CHURCH LEADERS CALL FOR END TO LATEST CONFLICT

CHILDREN BRUTALLY BEATEN BY CARERS

PLANET EARTH POISONED BY ITS OWN POLLUTION

HOMELESS IN CRISIS DURING COLD SNAP

ANGRY!

WHAT MAKES YOU ANGRY IN THE KINGDOM'S CAUSES?

JESUS CHRIST IS RAGING, RAGING IN THE STREETS
WHERE INJUSTICE SPIRALS AND ALL HOPE RETREATS.
LISTEN, LORD JESUS,
I AM ANGRY TOO;
IN THE KINGDOM'S CAUSES
LET ME RAGE WITH YOU.

(Taken from the song *Jesus Christ is waiting* by John L. Bell and Graham Maule, © 1988 WGRG, Iona Community)

IT MAKES ME ANGRY THAT...

FIFTH SUNDAY OF LENT

Thought for the day

Through Christ's death, full life would come to people of all nations and generations.

Readings

Jeremiah 31:31-34
Psalm 51:1-12 or Psalm 119:9-16
Hebrews 5:5-10
John 12:20-33

Aim

To look at the significance of the Gentiles coming to Jesus and hearing his teaching at this point.

Starter

Have some blotting paper and dampen it so they can watch a blob of colour from various dark-coloured felt-tip pens spreading out in all directions and revealing lots of hidden colours.

Teaching

Have the spreading blots displayed as you read the passage from Jeremiah, focusing on the opening-up of people's knowledge of God – '. . . all of them will know me, says the Lord.' Go on to look at John 12:20-22. As this Gospel is very condensed, it's best to take it in sections.

Explain that the Greeks were Gentiles, and John wants us to know that here are representatives from the 'other nations' seeking Jesus out. Take them briefly back to the wedding at Cana (John 2:3-5) where Jesus had said his hour had not yet come, and then read what Jesus says when he finds these Gentiles looking for him (John 12:23). Everyone can read this verse aloud together. This is the point in Jesus' ministry when the 'standby for action' lights start flashing. The big act of total self-giving has moved from the long-term planning stage to red alert, and, humanly speaking, Jesus' adrenaline starts pumping.

As he starts teaching them about what to expect (John 12:24-26) all the horror of what it will entail rushes into him, and John gives us a blow-by-blow account of Jesus, the Son of God, wrestling with the human temptation to scream, 'Stop! I can't go through with it!' (verse 27). What will happen? Wonderfully, Jesus manages to triumph in that battle, and chooses for God's name to be glorified, whatever the cost to himself (verse 28a).

We can imagine God the Father on the edge of his seat (so to speak) through Jesus' agonising, and now immediately he is there to affirm and comfort him, giving him a new surge of confidence, which we can hear in Jesus' voice in the last couple of verses (28b-33).

Praying

Father, may your name be glorified!
Whatever the cost,
may your will be done in me.

Activities

On the sheet they can trace the way Jesus has to go through this human temptation so that the self-giving is freely chosen, in full knowledge of the cost involved. This commitment is then related to their own lives and faith journey. They are also helped to see how the grain of wheat analogy works.

Discussion starters

1. How does it help that even Jesus shrank from the thought of the suffering ahead?

2. How is it that Jesus being lifted up (both when crucified and ascended) can draw all humanity to himself?

Notes

PALM SUNDAY

Thought for the day

As the Messiah, Jesus enters Jerusalem, knowing that he rides towards rejection and death in order to save his people.

Readings

Liturgy of the Palms:
Mark 11:1-11 or John 12:12-16
Psalm 118:1-2, 19-24

Liturgy of the Passion:
Isaiah 50:4-9a
Psalm 31:9-16
Philippians 2:5-11
Mark 14:1-15:47 or Mark 15:1-39 (40-47)

Aim

To look at why the Messiah had to suffer and die before he could rise in glory.

Starter

If possible, let the young people join in with the all-age procession, playing instruments, and carrying banners as they go. Or gather all the age groups and take them on a Palm Sunday procession, preferably outside. Take a portable tape player so they can all sing along with the songs. The banners read 'Jesus is the Christ' and 'Jesus is the Messiah'.

Teaching

Remind everyone of the way the prophets had known for many generations that God would one day send his chosen One, like a new King David, to save his people and reign for ever. The image they had of this Saviour was not all riding out to battle with the occupying army. Read from Isaiah 50, which is one of the passages about the suffering servant, noticing how the prophet senses the need for the Saviour to be despised and rejected as part of his saving work of love.

Notice the links with the story of the Passion, where we see Jesus in this suffering servant role. (Mark 14:1-15:47) Read the Passion with different voices for the different parts, with everyone reading the crowd parts. It is worthwhile to spend time on this.

Praying

Father's pure radiance, perfect in innocence,
yet learns obedience to death on a cross.
Suffering to give us life,
conquering through sacrifice,
and as they crucify prays: 'Father, forgive.'
O what a mystery, meekness and majesty.
Bow down and worship,
for this is your God.

(Taken from the song *Meekness and majesty* by Graham Kendrick © 1986 Kingsway's Thankyou Music)

Activities

There is space on the sheet this week to express the entry into Jerusalem with its welcome and praise, but with the shadow of the cross and its painful glory present.

Discussion starters

1. What do we discover about God's nature through the events of the Passion?

2. Why did the work of saving humanity have to end like this?

Notes

FATHER'S PURE RADIANCE, PERFECT IN INNOCENCE,
YET LEARNS OBEDIENCE TO DEATH ON A CROSS.
SUFFERING TO GIVE US LIFE, CONQUERING THROUGH
                                    SACRIFICE,
AND AS THEY CRUCIFY PRAYS: 'FATHER FORGIVE'.
O WHAT A MYSTERY, MEEKNESS AND MAJESTY.
BOW DOWN AND WORSHIP,
FOR THIS IS YOUR GOD.

(Taken from the song *Meekness and Majesty* by Graham Kendrick
© 1986 Kingsway's Thankyou Music)

HOSANNA !

WHY WERE THE CROWDS SO EXCITED?

They badly wanted to be free, and here was the Messiah coming into their city to be their king and lead them to freedom.

BUT JESUS WASN'T THAT SORT OF KING, WAS HE? I CAN'T IMAGINE HIM LEADING AN ARMY.

Exactly. His kingdom is not about one country. It's about the hearts of people being ruled by selfless love.

DRAW HOW THE ENTRY INTO JERUSALEM MUST HAVE FELT FOR JESUS, KNOWING WHAT WAS BOUND TO HAPPEN TO HIM —

— BE AS REALISTIC OR ABSTRACT AS YOU LIKE, TO EXPRESS THE FEELINGS!

WARFF!

EASTER

Easter Day

If possible, it is recommended that the children and young people are in church with the other age groups today. Use and adapt some of the all-age ideas from the *Living Stones* Complete Resource Book, and involve the young people in some of the music and in decorating the church.

Thought for the day

Jesus is alive; Love has won the victory over sin and death.

Readings

Acts 10:34-43 or Isaiah 25:6-9
Psalm 118:1-2, 14-24
1 Corinthians 15:1-11 or Acts 10:34-43
John 20:1-18 or Mark 16:1-8

Aim

To look at the accounts of the Resurrection and weigh up the evidence.

Starter

Spread out a whole pack of cards and ask one person to choose a card, without giving away which one is chosen. The rest of you are going to detect the right card by a process of elimination. The card chooser can only answer everyone's questions with a 'Yes' or 'No'. As each question is answered, turn over all the cards now eliminated, until the correct card is there, plain to see.

Teaching

As we are used to celebrating Easter every year, the shock and impossibility of the event can get glossed over and taken for granted. As you read the Gospel account today, ask them to imagine they are particular characters (tell them which before you read) so that during the reading they are thinking through that person's head. Afterwards talk to everyone in character about how they felt, and how their feelings changed.

The reading from Acts will give extra insight into Peter's character, as this is his own later account of what happened, once he's had plenty of time to think things over. Has his conviction changed or is he still convinced that Jesus is alive?

Talk over the possibilities of what really happened. It's important that these are looked at and not assumed to be rubbish. Could Jesus have not really died, but just collapsed and later recovered? Could the disciples have stolen the body? Could the disciples and the women have wanted to see Jesus and so imagined they saw him?

Look at these questions in the light of the accounts they have read, so they can see that the strange truth is actually more likely. (*Who moved the stone?* by Frank Morison (Bromley, 1983) can be recommended for any wanting to read further.) The facts and circumstances point to Jesus dying and rising to new life. What does that say about who Jesus was? And is?

Praying

The dead One lives
and the power of death is broken
by the power of Love.
O my Lord, this is an amazing truth,
and you are an amazing God!

Activities

There is a role-play to explore the thinking and fears of the disciples, and some information about the Resurrection events. They are encouraged to think about the difference a crucified and risen Christ makes to the way we spend the rest of our own life.

Discussion starters

1. What did the disciples gain from seeing Jesus after the Resurrection?

2. Since the Resurrection, Jesus is alive for all time, including today. Do we still tend to think of him in history? What evidence have we that Jesus is with us now?

Notes

SECOND SUNDAY OF EASTER

Thought for the day

Our faith in the risen Christ is bound to affect the way we live.

Readings

Acts 4:32-35
Psalm 133
1 John 1:1–2:2
John 20:19-31

Aim

To look at the stages of Thomas' journey to faith.

Starter

Give small groups clues to where the different components of a torch are. Each group races to be the first to assemble and light their torch. (Or you could have a tape player, lead, socket and tape to assemble.)

Teaching

Our torches only lit up once we had gathered all the pieces and fitted them together. That's also how Inspector Morse or any other detective works. Our questions and investigations help us put facts and experiences together to reach a conclusion. Today we watch this happening in Thomas, one of the disciples who very much wanted to believe Jesus was risen, but found it very difficult. Read today's Gospel. Faced with the impossibility of death turning into risen life, what makes Thomas believe?

Working with the text, go through the stages:

1. For some reason Thomas was not with the others – denial and avoidance strategy.
2. Thomas hears the stories of the others – witnesses heard.
3. Can it be true? – wavers but digs in to avoid being conned and insists on solid evidence.
4. Thomas joins the disciples same place, same time, a week later – takes a risk and puts himself in right place just in case.
5. Meets Jesus – finds that the meeting is more convincing than anything, solid proof no longer needed.

Finally read the passage from Acts to hear the faith in action.

Praying

Lord God, you hear my questions and my doubts –
they are all part of me seeking you;
lead me to a deeper understanding
of who you are and where we are going together.
Amen.

Activities

On the sheet there is a pictorial look at the early Church and how it showed Jesus' risen life. They are also helped to look at that breathing of 'beyond death' life, and how it still changes us now.

Discussion starters

1. Jesus breathes on his disciples the life which death cannot touch, the life of God's fullness. How does that change them?

2. What would you point to as evidence that Jesus is alive today, even though we cannot actually see him?

Notes

THIRD SUNDAY OF EASTER

Thought for the day

Having redeemed us by his death, Jesus can offer us the forgiveness of our sin, which sets us free to live.

Readings

Acts 3:12-19
Psalm 4
1 John 3:1-7
Luke 24:36b-48

Aim

To see the importance of spreading the news of forgiveness.

Starter

Cut out news headlines from their stories, and stick them around the room separately. Everyone goes round matching up the headline with the story.

Teaching

Begin with the Gospel – Luke's account of that Sunday evening encounter with the risen Jesus. Notice the similarities with last week's account, seeing how there is real fear registered at first, which Jesus carefully addresses. He doesn't even start telling them anything important until he is sure they are happy and at peace with him being there. It's the same now. We need to get used to spending quality time in Jesus' company if we are wanting him to help us understand things in life.

Now look at the passage from Acts, putting it briefly in context of the healing, and the crowd's enthusiasm to give Peter and John all the credit for it. Notice how they use the occasion to do what Jesus had told them to – telling people to change their lives, making them right with God and being set free by his forgiveness.

Finally look at the reading from 1 John, where the writer is still amazed and overjoyed by the way God's love changes lives. Again, the new life is tied up with whatever happens to us when we repent and are forgiven. It's something so good that it needs to be thoroughly investigated!

Praying

The King is among us, his Spirit is here,
let's draw near and worship, let songs fill the air.

(From a song by Graham Kendrick,
© 1981 Kingsway's Thankyou Music)

Activities

On the sheet they unpack the steps Jesus goes through to sort out the disciples, and the steps Peter goes through to sort out the way the crowd is thinking. They are encouraged to look at situations where we can choose to pocket the glory ourselves rather than giving it to God. There is also a look at taking up Jesus' commission to tell others the good news of forgiveness.

Discussion starters

1. Do we pass over serious, regular repentance, thinking of it only being really necessary for a few 'heavyweight' sins which we haven't committed?

2. Does living the risen life feel different, as the apostles claim? If it doesn't, could it be we aren't living it yet?

Notes

FOURTH SUNDAY OF EASTER

Thought for the day

'I am the Good Shepherd and I lay down my life for the sheep.'

Readings

Acts 4:5-12
Psalm 23
1 John 3:16-24
John 10:11-18

Aim

To look at how Jesus takes on himself the role of the Good Shepherd.

Starter

Role-call. Give out identities to particular people, which they keep secret. Then provide a situation which they all act out in role. Onlookers have to guess the identities/characters from the way they are acting. (Example – travelling on a train: someone with chicken pox, a spy, a *Sun* reporter looking for a story, and the Queen travelling incognito.)

Teaching

Jesus knew the scriptures and what had been written about the Messiah in the books of the prophets, and the Psalms. There was quite a lot about God's shepherding (read Psalm 23) and the Messiah would be a kind of Shepherd King, like David. (Have a look at a few examples, such as 2 Samuel 5:2; Psalm 28:9; Ezekiel 34:16; Isaiah 40:11.) There was also a recurring theme of the false shepherding of God's people, who were left as sheep without a shepherd (Ezekiel 34:5). In Mark and Matthew, Jesus is said to have compassion on the people because of this (Matthew 9:36 and Mark 6:34).

Often the leaders of God's people are criticised for their unshepherdlike behaviour (Jeremiah 10:21; Ezekiel 34:2; Isaiah 56:11).

So now, with this background, look at today's Gospel, John 10:11-18. Jesus is not only showing his disciples the example of the real shepherds around on the hills where they were living. He is also directing them to see how he is fulfilling the prophets and the Psalms as the real, authentic leader of God's people, in contrast to those who are only out for themselves, and are not listening carefully to God.

Praying

The Lord is my shepherd; I shall not be in want.
He makes me lie down in green pastures
and leads me beside still waters.
He revives my soul
and guides me along right pathways
for his name's sake.
Though I walk through the valley
of the shadow of death,
I shall fear no evil;
for you are with me;
your rod and your staff comfort me.
You spread a table for me
in the sight of those who trouble me;
you have anointed my head with oil,
and my cup is running over.
Surely your goodness and mercy shall follow me
all the days of my life,
and I will dwell in the house of the Lord for ever.

(Psalm 23)

Activities

On the sheet there is a picture of a hired shepherd fleeing in danger, and they are helped to explore this symbol in terms of leadership of God's people, and our own Christian witness. They also look at why Peter and John were imprisoned.

Discussion starters

1. Does our lack of trust in the Good Shepherd and our lack of expectation prevent his work being done?

2. How has God redeemed unpromising events in your life (as individuals and as a church) and turned them into good opportunities?

Notes

GULP – I'M OFF!

Why are Israel's spiritual leaders accused of being like this?

Jeremiah 10:21
Ezekiel 34:2
Isaiah 56:11

BAAAA !!!

GOTCHA!

How does our own Christian caring measure up?

They might tease me.

I don't want to look silly.

I need all my money to spend on me!

I want a nice, easy life.

'I AM THE GOOD SHEPHERD'

WHY DID JESUS SAY HE WAS THE 'GOOD' SHEPHERD? All those listening to Jesus knew that only the shepherds who really cared for the sheep would bother to take risks for them.

AND JESUS IS A RISK-TAKING SHEPHERD?
Yes. Jesus knows us really well, and loves us.

WHAT ABOUT LAYING DOWN HIS LIFE FOR US – IT SOUNDS AS IF JESUS COULD HAVE CHOSEN NOT TO BE KILLED.
That's right. He could have called on all heaven's powers to get down from that cross and walk away.

BUT THEN HE WOULDN'T HAVE SAVED US, WOULD HE? No.

THE LORD IS MY SHEPHERD; I SHALL NOT BE IN WANT.
HE MAKES ME LIE DOWN IN GREEN PASTURES
AND LEADS ME BESIDE STILL WATERS.
HE REVIVES MY SOUL AND GUIDES ME ALONG RIGHT
PATHWAYS FOR HIS NAME'S SAKE.
THOUGH I WALK THROUGH THE VALLEY OF THE SHADOW
OF DEATH I SHALL FEAR NO EVIL;
FOR YOU ARE WITH ME; YOUR ROD AND YOUR STAFF
COMFORT ME.
YOU SPREAD A TABLE FOR ME IN THE SIGHT
OF THOSE WHO TROUBLE ME;
YOU HAVE ANOINTED MY HEAD WITH OIL,
AND MY CUP IS RUNNING OVER.
SURELY YOUR GOODNESS AND MERCY SHALL
FOLLOW ME ALL THE DAYS OF MY LIFE,
AND I WILL DWELL IN THE HOUSE OF THE LORD
FOR EVER.
— PSALM 23 —

BECAUSE THEY WERE TELLING EVERYONE THAT...

WHY WERE PETER AND JOHN IN PRISON?

ACTS 4:2-12

Fifth Sunday of Easter

Thought for the day

To produce fruit we need to be joined on to the true vine.

Readings

Acts 8:26-40
Psalm 22:25-31
1 John 4:7-21
John 15:1-8

Aim

To understand the importance of us being 'joined on' to Jesus if we are to produce any fruit spiritually.

Starter

Provide a length of wire, a torch battery and bulb, and make the bulb light up.

Teaching

As the season of Easter continues, we're reading the book of Acts of the Apostles, looking at the different ways in which the good news spread. We've seen how miracles of healing landed Peter and John in trouble with the authorities and gave them good opportunities to witness to the risen Jesus, and now we read about Philip, who is led to a desert road to Ethiopia.

Read the passage from Acts together, looking at the stages Philip goes through with the Ethiopian, which link up once again with Jesus' example:

- listening expectantly to God and co-operating right away
- listening to where the Ethiopian is spiritually at the moment
- answering the Ethiopian's questions
- leading him on from here using the scriptures with which he is familiar
- helping him see the truth about Jesus

And this is a very good model for all of us when spreading the good news.

Philip was producing a rich harvest of spiritual fruit, and he was able to because he was constantly connected to Jesus. Jesus had talked about how important this was in the Gospel for today. Read this now.

How can we make sure we are part of the true vine? Look at being baptised, daily prayer and Bible reading, coming to worship regularly with the other people of God, and committing our life direction to match up with the will of God.

Praying

Breathe on me, Breath of God,
fill me with life anew,
that I may love what thou dost love,
and do what thou wouldst do.

Activities

On the sheet the teaching about Philip and the Ethiopian is reinforced, and they are encouraged to check their own position on (or off) the true vine, reviewing how their practice matches up with where they want to be.

Discussion starters

1. How can we check that we are still firmly attached to the true vine?

2. Does belonging to the true vine mean that we have to sacrifice our independence?

Notes

IN NEED OF PRUNING →

FRUIT PRODUCING

CUT OFF AND DEAD

PRUNED AND ALL SET TO GROW WELL

JESUS

WHERE ARE YOU?

I AM THE TRUE VINE

IS THAT ANOTHER WAY OF SAYING 'LIVE IN ME AND I WILL LIVE IN YOU'?

Yes. It's a good picture of the way Jesus' life fills our life, so that we can live lovingly.

SO JESUS NEEDS US AS WELL AS US NEEDING HIM?

That's right. We work together. Your words and hands and feet can bring God's love to the places *you* go and the people *you* meet.

WHAT IF WE TRY TO GO IT ALONE?

Soon the stocks run out. That's why we need to be joined on to the living supply which keeps renewing and refilling us.

CHECKLIST 1

ARE YOU GROWING IN ANY OF THESE?

love ❏ joy ❏ peace ❏
patience ❏ kindness ❏
goodness ❏
faithfulness ❏
gentleness ❏
self-control ❏

CHECKLIST 2

ARE YOU DOING ANY OF THESE EACH DAY?

talking to God ❏
listening to God ❏
wanting to live God's way ❏
reading your Bible ❏
thanking God ❏

Why did Philip hitch a lift with an Ethiopian official?

_____

_____

_____

What was the Ethiopian reading?

_____

_____

What do you think Philip said to help the Ethiopian understand what he was reading?

_____

_____

_____

BREATHE ON ME, BREATH OF GOD,
FILL ME WITH LIFE ANEW,
THAT I MAY LOVE
WHAT THOU DOST LOVE,
AND DO
WHAT THOU WOULDST DO.

JERUSALEM   GAZA

Sixth Sunday of Easter

Thought for the day

We are to love one another as Jesus loves us.

Readings

Acts 10:44-48
Psalm 98
1 John 5:1-6
John 15:9-17

Aim

To look at what it means to be Jesus' friends.

Starter

Either use the sketch on page 127 or play a co-operative game such as making a circle of everyone sitting on the lap of the person in front, or telling a story in which each person in the circle adds a word.

Teaching

Begin by reading today's Gospel, which follows on from last week's picture of the vine and branches. Bear in mind when Jesus was saying these things – shortly before his arrest and death. Ask them to pick out particular phrases that seem specially important, or which surprise them. Being Jesus' friends looks as if it brings both honour and responsibility. What are these? (That we have the privilege of working co-operatively with the living God; that we are to love one another as Jesus loves us.)

Now look at 1 John 5:1-6, particularly verses 3-4. Make it clear that we are not obeying his commands in order for him to like us. It's God's love for us which makes us love him and want to live like him.

Finally look at an example of co-operative friendship with Jesus – Peter going along with God's will even though it's not what he might have chosen to do on his own, with the result that all those people receive the Holy Spirit and the freedom that gives.

Praying

(To pray regularly throughout each day)

Here I am, Lord,
ready to work with you.
Show me how I can share your love
here . . . now.

Activities

On the sheet they are helped to explore how Jesus loves us, and what that is going to mean for us loving one another. They are also looking at the way we are chosen and appointed to go and bear fruit – both the honour and the responsibility.

Discussion starters

1. Jesus once observed that it is those who have been forgiven much who love much. Do we feel fully forgiven, with the rush of love that produces, or has the penny yet to drop?

2. Imagine walking through a normal day, meeting the usual people and problems, but in the knowledge of God's love and forgiveness, and literally loving as Jesus loves us. What would it be like, and how would it differ from how we usually live?

Notes

Seventh Sunday of Easter

Thought for the day

Although now hidden from our sight, Jesus lives for ever, and in him we can live the Resurrection life even while we are on earth.

Readings

Acts 1:15-17, 21-26
Psalm 1
1 John 5:9-13
John 17:6-19

Aim

To look at what it means to live in Jesus and live the risen life.

Starter

Two teams (or more for larger numbers) sit facing each other, about a metre apart. The aim is to hit a balloon behind the other team's chairs.

Teaching

If no one has been involved in Ascension, include it now by starting the Acts reading from verse 9. Point out that Peter feels it is a matter of urgency to choose a replacement for Judas, and part of their preparation for receiving the gift of the Holy Spirit. They are putting everything in order, ready for the new life. Notice, too, how God's choice is what matters, not anyone else's. We can learn from this to get our lives facing the right direction in readiness for God to act in them, and actively to want God's will in all the choices and decisions we make each day.

If possible read 1 John 5:9-13 from *The Message* as this makes it clearer and more accessible to them. Draw their attention particularly to the words, 'God gave us eternal life; the life is in his Son. So, whoever has the Son, has life; whoever rejects the Son, rejects life.'

Now read John 17:6-19. Jesus is praying for all of us who live as his followers in the world, knowing how difficult it will sometimes be for us, but not praying for us to be taken out of the dangers because the work we are doing is so vital; it needs doing. It is reassuring for us to know that whenever we are talking about our faith, or standing up for what is right, or helping someone else to think through their faith, Jesus is there praying for us and, through him, God's life is there in us, giving us the words to say, and the courage to do the work.

Praying

O come to my heart, Lord Jesus,
there is room in my heart for thee.

Activities

On the sheet they are encouraged to join the disciples in their waiting on God during this coming week, asking for a fresh outpouring of the Holy Spirit. And they are helped to look at any preparation in their own lives which needs to be done.

Discussion starters

1. In what way are we 'one', in spite of the different labels and packaging?

2. How can we, who live two thousand years after Christ, be considered 'witnesses'?

Notes

THE WAITING GAME ...

		Read	Pray	Do
TODAY	To read: Acts 1:9-26 To pray: The Lord's Prayer To do: Choose a time to pray each day this week			
MONDAY	To read: John 16:7a To pray: This week's prayer To do: Notice how the wind affects things			
TUESDAY	To read: John 14:15-18 To pray: This week's prayer To do: Light a candle and watch the flame			
WEDNESDAY	To read: John 14:25-26 To pray: This week's prayer To do: Sit still and notice your breathing			
THURSDAY	To read: John 14:27 To pray: This week's prayer To do: As you breathe air into your body, think of yourself breathing God's life into your spirit.			
FRIDAY	To read: John 17:25-26 To pray: This week's prayer To do: Be kind to someone you don't like			
SATURDAY	To read: John 20:28-31 To pray: This week's prayer To do: Notice 10 signs of God's love today			

THE DAY OF PENTECOST

LIVING THE RISEN LIFE

HOW COULD THE DISCIPLES LIVE THE RISEN LIFE? IT WAS JESUS WHO DID THAT, NOT THEM.

You're right. But one of the things Jesus promised was that soon after he had gone away from them into heaven, they'd be able to share his risen life.

HOW?

God's Spirit would come to them and so they would have God's eternal life living in them.

WOULD THAT STOP THEM DYING?

It would stop them finishing at death. Life would then carry on in a whole new dimension.

SO THIS RISEN LIFE IS LIKE LIVING ETERNALLY EVEN BEFORE WE'VE PHYSICALLY DIED?

Yes. Life in all its fullness.

O COME TO MY HEART, LORD JESUS, THERE IS ROOM IN MY HEART FOR THEE.

ANY CLEARING OR CLEANING THAT NEEDS DOING TO MAKE MORE ROOM HERE?

My way

money

If only...

HAVE WE GOT ROOM IN OUR HEARTS FOR JESUS TO COME IN POWER, OR ARE WE CLUTTERED UP WITH OTHER JUNK?

Bad habits

How do I look?

It's not fair

PENTECOST

Thought for the day

The Holy Spirit of God is poured out in power on the expectant disciples, just as Jesus promised.

Readings

Acts 2:1-21 or Ezekiel 37:1-14
Psalm 104:24-34, 35b
Romans 8:22-27 or Acts 2:1-21
John 15:26-27; 16:4b-15

Aim

To look at how the coming of the Holy Spirit affected the disciples and affects Jesus' followers now.

Starter

All change! Have a selection of scarves and hats, enough for everyone and as silly as you like. Use a CD player for music so that you can skip from track to track. When the music starts, each person dresses up. Whenever the track changes, they have to swap their hat and scarf with someone else.

Teaching

Explain that the disciples had seen a lot of changes in the last few years of their lives. Jesus had called them out of their normal jobs, they'd travelled around to different places, changed their way of thinking and their way of thinking about God. They'd lived through the crucifixion, Jesus being dead and Jesus being alive again. Now they were waiting for another change, not quite knowing what the Holy Spirit would do to them, but knowing it was important to be ready for it.

Now read from Acts. Consider having this reading prepared on tape, either from a professional recording, or using a couple of adults from the congregation, and adding the sound of the wind, or some music. Then look up the quoted passage from Joel, so they can see where it comes from.

What has happened to the disciples with the coming of the Holy Spirit? How are they behaving? How are they different? Why are they so excited? What was it they wanted everyone to know?

Praying

Lord, that power the disciples were given –
I want it, too.
I've seen the way they were changed
and strengthened – and I want that, too.
Will you let your Holy Spirit
come to me and fill my life?

Activities

There is a short sketch to start them looking at the possibility of the Holy Spirit changing things still, today and here. And they are encouraged to learn how to wait on God, both privately and as a group, so that they grow in his Spirit.

Discussion starters

1. Why isn't the Holy Spirit poured out more than it is in our own church? What can we learn from the disciples' expectant waiting?

2. Do we try to impose restrictions or guidelines for the Holy Spirit in case our lives are too much challenged by too much of God's presence?

Notes

THE HOLY SPIRIT OF GOD

WHAT REALLY HAPPENED? WAS THERE A STORM WITH LIGHTNING OR SOMETHING?

Those who were there said it sounded like a rushing wind and they sensed brightness rather like flames. But it was not actual wind and fire. The onlookers came running to see what had happened.

I SUPPOSE GOD'S POWER IS BOUND TO BE SPECTACULAR LIKE THAT.

Not always. Sometimes the Spirit comes very gently, giving a sense of deep peace and calm.

CAN THE HOLY SPIRIT STILL COME TO US TODAY?

It can and it does!

Beth: Have you noticed how Dave's changed over the last few months?

Ryan: Yes, I have. He seems more settled. And he doesn't keep losing his temper.

Carl: He lost it last week though.

Ryan: Yeah, but that was when he got mad at Ross for kicking my shirt into the gutter.

Beth: In the old days it would have been Dave doing the shirt kicking!

Carl: What's happened, do you reckon?

Ryan: Well, we've all been praying for him, haven't we? And he's been asking questions about things as well.

Beth: What things?

Ryan: Oh, you know – who made God . . . what are ghosts . . . that kind of stuff.

Carl: God's amazing. Fancy him listening to our prayers.

Beth: Yes, and he's sorting Dave out. God's power is so incredible.

All: God does things. God ACTS TOO.

Carl: Acts 2! That's today's reading!

HOW TO GET IN ON THE ACTS!

Learn how to wait on the living, real God, making yourself still and quiet, and attentive

Expect God to act

Read the book of Acts straight through, to see God at work in his friends

Want God's kingdom to come and God's will to be done

Live thankfully

LORD, THAT POWER THE DISCIPLES WERE GIVEN – I WANT IT, TOO. I'VE SEEN THE WAY THEY WERE CHANGED AND STRENGTHENED – AND I WANT THAT, TOO. WILL YOU LET YOUR HOLY SPIRIT COME TO ME AND FILL MY LIFE?

ORDINARY TIME

TRINITY SUNDAY

Thought for the day

The mysterious and holy nature of the one true God is beyond our understanding, but it is both communal harmony and individual personality, Father, Son and Holy Spirit.

Readings

Isaiah 6:1-8
Psalm 29
Romans 8:12-17
John 3:1-17

Aim

To explore the nature of the Trinity.

Starter

Who are you? The group is going to discover as much as possible about you in five minutes. Before the timing starts, let them collectively establish what they do know about you already, so the question time isn't wasted. Explain that if you don't want to answer a particular question you will say so; but they can ask whatever they want to in order to get to know who you are and what you are like.

Teaching

Look back at how the group discovered more about you. They ran their minds over what they knew already and went on from there. Were there some things they thought they knew which turned out to be mistaken? Were they surprised by any of the new discoveries?

Today, on Trinity Sunday, we are focusing on who God is and what he is like. Collectively as a Church, over the years, some clear truths about God have been discovered:

• God is One Being

• God is Three Persons – Father, Son and Holy Spirit.

(Trinity means Tri-Unity, or Three in One and One in Three.)

Why does the Church describe God in this way? Look together at what they know of God as Father, Son and Spirit, to see how the concept of Trinity has developed, referring to these passages to help: Genesis 1:1-3; Isaiah 9:6; Luke 1:35; John 10:36-38; John 14:25-26.

Finally read John 3:1-17 to see how the invisible nature of the wind helps Nicodemus discover more about the nature of God.

Praying

Holy, holy, holy is the Lord Almighty;
the whole earth is full of his glory!

Activities

On the sheet there are aspects of the natural world which can help us understand more about the nature of God: the wind; infinity of space; simplicity/complexity of life structures; light; physical laws and order.

Discussion starters

1. How does each Person of the Trinity testify to the others?

2. What would you like God to enable you to 'see'?

Notes

WHAT CAN WE LEARN ABOUT GOD FROM THESE?

THE INVISIBLE WIND

3 IN 1 AND 1 IN 3

WHAT ON EARTH DOES ALL THAT MEAN? IT SOUNDS LIKE MATHS.

Well, it's what the word Trinity really means – Tri/Unity.

HOW CAN GOD BE ONE IF HE'S THREE?

You may well ask! With human brains we can't grasp all that Almighty God is, but we *do* know that he is the Father, the Son and the Holy Spirit, and yet remains the one and only true God.

THE INFINITY OF SPACE

LIGHT AND THE PHYSICAL LAWS

$E = mc^2$

SIMPLICITY / COMPLEXITY OF LIFE STRUCTURES

AND THESE...

GENESIS 1:1–3

JOHN 10:36–38

ISAIAH 9:6

LUKE 1:35

JOHN 14:25–26

HOLY, HOLY, HOLY IS THE LORD ALMIGHTY; THE WHOLE EARTH IS FULL OF HIS GLORY!

PROPER 4

Sunday between 29 May and 4 June inclusive
(if after Trinity Sunday)

Thought for the day

Jesus has the words of eternal life – he sheds light on a right attitude to the Law.

Readings

1 Samuel 3:1-10 (11-20) or Deuteronomy 5:12-15
Psalm 139:1-6, 13-18 or Psalm 81:1-10
2 Corinthians 4:5-12
Mark 2:23-3:6

Aim

To explore the nature of the Law and Jesus' interpretation of it.

Starter

Using a softball play French cricket. The batsperson stands in the centre with the others in a circle, passing the ball and throwing it to aim at the batsperson's legs. If they hit them, they take a turn in the centre.

Teaching

First read the passage from Deuteronomy 5, and have a brief look at the ten commandments, which are on the sheet. The spirit of the whole Law is love for God and love for neighbour, and in an effort to protect them and uphold them well, the teachers of the Law had got hung up on all the details and had lost sight of the real spirit of the Law.

Now go on to read today's Gospel, looking out for the way Jesus is going to deal with this over-zealous keeping of the letter of the Law, while shutting out the loving spirit of it. At what level are the teachers correct about Jesus breaking the Law, and at what level are they mistaken? Notice how Jesus doesn't draw away from doing what is right, even when it makes him dangerously unpopular with the authorities; never does he compromise God's values in order to protect his position.

Finally look at 2 Corinthians 4:5-12. In a way it interprets Jesus' actions in the Gospel, showing how he shines God's light in our hearts so that we can understand God better. That is bound to affect the way we live. It should prevent us getting so set in our ways and traditions that we stop bothering to listen to God's directing; it should give us an ideal by which to measure our attitudes to those in need.

Praying

Lord God, teach us your ways
of compassion and mercy,
so that the way we treat others
may be in line with the way you treat us.
Amen.

Activities

On the sheet there are the ten commandments and Jesus' summary of the Law, to use as a daily guide for right attitudes and behaviour. There is also space to put down all the present involvement of the parish with caring outreach. Any gaps can be noted and prayed about regularly, with ideas for action taken seriously.

Discussion starters

1. 'Love God and do what you like.' Is this a helpful way of looking at the Commandments, or should we be taking the actual laws more seriously than we do?

2. What do you think might horrify Jesus today and need his teaching about a drastic re-think?

Notes

THE TEN COMMANDMENTS

1. You shall have no other gods besides me.

2. Do not make or worship idols.

3. Don't take God's name and use it as a swear word.

4. Keep the Sabbath day holy and as a day of rest.

5. Honour your father and mother.

6. You shall not murder.

7. You shall not commit adultery.

8. You shall not steal.

9. You shall not give false witness against your neighbour.

10. You shall not long for others' possessions.

ALL OF WHICH CAN BE SUMMARISED AS:

LOVE GOD AND LOVE ONE ANOTHER

... ARE WE?

WHAT GOD'S LAW IS ALL ABOUT

HOW COULD THE TEACHERS OF THE LAW THINK IT WAS WRONG FOR JESUS TO HEAL THE MAN?

Look at No. 4 commandment.

BUT JESUS WAS DOING GOOD AND SETTING THE MAN FREE.

Exactly. He wanted to show the teachers that the Law is to help us, but not imprison us.

I THINK IT'S JUST AS HARD TO LOVE GOD AND ONE ANOTHER.

Yes, if we really lived by those rules, what other rules would we need?

MAKE A NOTE OF ALL THE CARING OUTREACH IN YOUR CHURCH.

MAKE A NOTE OF THE NEEDS OF THE COMMUNITY.

WHAT ARE THE GAPS?

WHAT NEEDS ARE THERE IN YOUR AREA?

LORD GOD, TEACH US YOUR WAYS OF COMPASSION AND MERCY, SO THAT THE WAY WE TREAT OTHERS MAY BE IN LINE WITH THE WAY YOU TREAT US. —AMEN—

PROPER 5

Sunday between 5 and 11 June inclusive
(if after Trinity Sunday)

Thought for the day

Anyone who does God's will is considered a close family member of Jesus.

Readings

1 Samuel 8:4-11 (12-15) 16-20 (11:14-15) or
Genesis 3:8-15
Psalm 138 or Psalm 130
2 Corinthians 4:13-5:1
Mark 3:20-35

Aim

To look at the scribes' accusations and Jesus' response.

Starter

Play 'netball' using a blow-up beach ball and a bucket or bin for the net. Play first with even sides, and then with everyone on the same side, and no opponents. Compare the scores!

Teaching

It is so much easier to score goals when we don't have any opposition! Today we are going to look at some opposition Jesus was faced with, and how he dealt with it.

It wasn't just when Jesus was around that people hit against God's way of love. Read the passage from Genesis to see that, right from the beginning, people have been self-willed, and their sin creates a rift between themselves and God; they no longer feel comfortable in his company. That is just as true now; we only feel comfortable in God's company when we are choosing to face his way and are being honest with him. Otherwise we try to hide from him, and avoid his company.

Now read today's Gospel, looking out for any friction and opposition to his work. There are two main areas in this reading – the accusation of the scribes, and the concerned family, coming to 'take charge' of Jesus.

What do the scribes accuse Jesus of doing? (Casting out demons by the power of demons.) Would this make logical sense? How does Jesus respond to what they are saying about him? (If Satan was fighting against himself in that way, his power would crash.) Logic proves that Jesus cannot be in league with Satan if he is overcoming evil spirits in people.

What about his family – why have they come, and why doesn't Jesus rush off home with them as they would like? Having heard the reports of the crowds surrounding Jesus all the time, giving him no time even to eat, and all the casting-out of evil spirits, they are anxious for him and don't understand that his work on earth is very important, and needs to be done, even if it's sometimes dangerous. He can't spend his life living quietly at home with his immediate family, or the saving work would not get done.

Sometimes families have to share their loved ones with a wider circle of people, and Jesus wants to include as close family all those who are doing their best to live God's way. That is the 'family likeness' which marks many people out to be members of Jesus' family.

Praying

Make me a channel of your peace.
Where there is hatred, let me bring your love.
Where there is injury, your pardon, Lord,
and where there's doubt, true faith in you.

(Taken from the song by Sebastian Temple,
based on the Prayer of St Francis
© 1967 OCP Publications, USA)

Activities

On the sheet there is space to put in an imagined subscript of Jesus' family, in order to put Jesus' reply in context. They can also draw a cartoon to get at the meaning of the scribes' accusations and Jesus' response. Some comments by those struggling with family expectations and God's calling can be used as discussion starters.

Discussion starters

1. It is quite an honour to be considered Jesus' close relatives! Do we behave as if this is true? Do we show any family likenesses?

2. What does it mean in practical terms to pray to God our Father: 'Let your will be done on earth as it is done in heaven'?

Notes

THE OPPOSITION

WHAT WERE THE SCRIBES SAYING ABOUT JESUS?

That he could only drive out demons from people because he was in league with Satan.

SO THEY WERE SAYING HIS POWER WASN'T GOOD BUT EVIL?

That's right.

BUT THAT WOULD BE LIKE SCORING AN OWN GOAL!

Exactly. Jesus pointed that out – if Satan was working against himself like that he would collapse.

HOW WAS JESUS REALLY ABLE TO DRIVE OUT DEMONS?

With God's power of total goodness and love. Evil is no match for that.

PROPER 6

Sunday between 12 and 18 June inclusive
(if after Trinity Sunday)

Thought for the day

From small beginnings, and by God's power, the kingdom of heaven grows.

Readings

1 Samuel 15:34-16:13 or Ezekiel 17:22-24
Psalm 20 or Psalm 92:1-4, 12-15
2 Corinthians 5:6-10 (11-13) 14-17
Mark 4:26-34

Aim

To look at Jesus' teaching on the growth of the kingdom of heaven.

Starter

If you have one of those Christmas ornaments where lit candles make angels move round and round, this is ideal for them to set up and watch, working out what keeps the movement going. Other appropriate 'machines' would be lamps where globules of oil float gracefully up and down, driven by the heat, or kites.

Teaching

First have a look at the Old Testament passage chosen for today. If it is the Samuel passage, use different voices and a narrator. If Ezekiel, explain first that King Nebuchadnezzar had taken the important people of Israel off into Babylon, and the prophet had described this as a great eagle tearing off the top branches of a cedar tree and planting it in a land of traders. Now, in contrast to the worldly way of doing things, we look at God's way of renewing and redeeming a hopeless situation.

With both readings, bring out the point that God decides what he will do and does it, for greatest good. We are called to work with him, rather than just following our own whims and fancies; the important thing is to check constantly with God what his will actually is. That way we will be less likely to find ourselves working in opposition to God.

Now read Mark 4:26-34. Look out for where the growing power lies. (Farmers and gardeners don't create the growth themselves, but work with the creative God to allow God's natural growing power to happen.) God can't *only* work where we are busying about his business. If we do our best to

provide the best conditions for people's faith to grow, the actual growth of the kingdom is going to happen through the loving God's power and will.

Finally look at this week's section of 2 Corinthians. Whether we are in this life or the next, our only goal is to please God. It is the love of Christ in us that controls us, enabling us to live fruitfully – his freely given gift rather than our hard work.

Praying

It is a good thing to give thanks to the Lord,
and to sing praises to your name, O Most High;
to tell of your loving kindness early in the morning
and of your faithfulness in the night season.

(From Psalm 92)

Activities

There is a short sketch on the sheet about a sun-bathing farmer who is busy growing his crop, and they are encouraged to explore the quiet, hidden growing of the kingdom of God. There is also a checklist for looking at signs of spiritual growing, both as individuals and in their church community.

Discussion starters

1. Do we sometimes block God's growing kingdom by wanting it to happen in a particular way for us, our family, or our church?

2. Is it possible to work too hard for the coming of the kingdom?

Notes

- Excuse me, but shouldn't you be working? I mean . . . you're a farmer, aren't you?

- Uh? . . . Oh . . . working! Should I be working? What do you mean – I AM working!

- But here you are, sunbathing! How can that be work?

- Well, I assure you I'm working very hard! I'm growing oats, wheat and barley at the moment.

- Oh, yeah? Then they can't be growing very well if you're here snoozing, can they?

- Ah, well, that's just where you're wrong! I planted those seeds, right? And now they're growing – whether I'm watching them at it or not! You just come back in a month and see for yourself!

SO ... HOW DOES THE KINGDOM GROW?

IT IS A GOOD THING TO GIVE
THANKS TO THE LORD,
AND TO SING PRAISES TO
YOUR NAME, O MOST HIGH;
TO TELL OF YOUR LOVING
KINDNESS EARLY IN THE MORNING
AND OF YOUR FAITHFULNESS
IN THE NIGHT SEASON.
(— FROM PSALM 92 —)

GOD'S KINGDOM GROWS

IS JESUS SAYING WE DON'T NEED TO DO ANYTHING TO HELP THE KINGDOM GROW?

No, but he's reminding us that the actual growing is God's business, and it happens.

SO IS OUR JOB TO GET THE GROUND READY AND KEEP IT FREE OF RUBBLE AND WEEDS?

Yes! We work with God on that, and planting the seed. Then God can bring those seeds to harvest.

I SUPPOSE IT'S A BIT POMPOUS TO THINK IT'S ALL DOWN TO OUR HARD WORK.

Yes – a bit like a driver thinking he makes a car go along.

SIGNS OF KINGDOM GROWTH?

I think the signs to look for would be ...

1	2
3	4

Can you see them?

Here	1	2	3	4
In yourself				
In your church community				
In our society				

PROPER 7

Sunday between 19 and 25 June inclusive
(if after Trinity Sunday)

Thought for the day

What kind of person is this? Even the wind and waves obey him.

Readings

1 Samuel 17:(1a, 4-11, 19-23) 32-49 or
1 Samuel 17:57-18:5, 10-16 or Job 38:1-11
Psalm 9:9-20 or Psalm 133 or Psalm 107:1-3, 23-32
2 Corinthians 6:1-13
Mark 4:35-41

Aim

To explore the implications of the calming of the storm.

Starter

What are we? Explain that they are some kind of group with some kind of leader, and they can work out what they are by asking the leader questions (yes/no answers only). They may be objects, animals or people, or a combination. To start them off they are given one clue.

Here are some possible scenarios:

- A group of planes at different flying levels, waiting to be given permission to land from ground control. (Clue: boiled sweets and travel wrist bands/travel pills)

- Swallows perched on a telegraph wire gathering in the autumn for their leader to set them off on migration to Africa. (Clue: a feather)

- Members of a morris dance team with the leader playing an accordion. (Clue: bells and a white hanky)

- A mountain rescue team in thick fog on Snowdon guided by the compass. (Clue: A map and a first aid kit)

Teaching

What does it mean for God to be in charge? First read the chosen Old Testament passage, looking at it from this point of view. Notice what it does and doesn't mean – responsible loving, picking up pieces, drawing together and planning, yet following natural laws and allowing us the freedom of choice.

Now read from Mark's Gospel the account of Jesus calming the wind and waves.

Why do they think the disciples woke Jesus up?

Do they think they would all have drowned if Jesus hadn't commanded the weather to calm down?

Why might Jesus have chosen to do this instead of comforting the disciples and cheering them through the difficult situation? (Feeling compassion for them/showing a sign?/fighting with evil?)

What did it help the disciples to understand about Jesus in a very dramatic lesson?

What does it help us to see about Jesus as we read the account nearly two thousand years later?

Share ideas and other questions they may have.

Praying

Lead us, heavenly Father, lead us
o'er the world's tempestuous sea.
Guard us, guide us, keep us, feed us,
for we have no help but thee.
Yet possessing every blessing
if our God our Father be.

Activities

On the sheet there are some of the questions people ask about God intervening, and hints and references are given to help them work out possible answers. They are also invited to look at possible storms into which Jesus speaks calm – in their own lives, in the Church and in the news. This can all lead on to prayer and action.

Discussion starters

1. When were you last stunned by the awesome power of the living God? Share your experiences and how they affected your understanding of God.

2. If people know something of what God is really like, how is it likely to affect the way they pray?

Notes

PROPER 8

Sunday between 26 June and 2 July inclusive

Thought for the day

God's power can reach even into death and draw out life.

Readings

2 Samuel 1:1, 17-27 or
Wisdom of Solomon 1:13-15; 2:23-24
Psalm 130 or Psalm 30 or Lamentations 3:23-33
2 Corinthians 8:7-15
Mark 5:21-43

(Lamentations 3:23-33 may be read as the first reading in place of the Wisdom passage.)

Aim

To explore the implications of this healing from death.

Starter

Use a stopwatch and set someone off talking for one minute on a particular subject. They can be interrupted and challenged for repetitions or hesitations, after which the challenger continues the talk. Whoever is talking at time-up is the winner.

Teaching

Putting the reading in context, look first at 1 Samuel 1, and talk a little together about how sad it is when someone we know and love dies, and how we miss seeing them. You may also like to look at the passage from Lamentations.

Now make a point of moving from the Old to the New Testament, and find Mark's Gospel. Read this with different voices taking the various parts. Are they surprised at Jesus actually raising the dead? What does this show his followers? Why do they think only a few were allowed to be present?

Also look at the healing which takes place on the way to Jairus' house. How do they think Jairus might have been feeling while Jesus took time to talk to the woman? How do they cope with urgent interruptions? What if the interruption was the reason the little girl was already dead – might this be why Jesus was prepared to bring her back from the dead?

Finally look at what Mark shows us about faith. Where does faith and believing come up in the two healings of today's Gospel? What does Jesus say about it?

Praying

Be still, for the power of the Lord
is moving in this place;
he comes to cleanse and heal, to minister his grace.
No work too hard for him,
in faith receive from him.
Be still, for the power of the Lord
is moving in this place.

(Taken from the song *Be still, for the presence* by David J. Evans, © 1986 Kingsway's Thankyou Music)

Activities

There is a role-play on the sheet to help them see today's Gospel from various different standpoints, and there is space for them to record what this account reveals of the nature of Jesus and his mission.

Discussion starters

1. The situation in the Gospel of urgent business being interrupted by another crisis is all too familiar! What can we learn from Jesus' way of dealing with it?

2. Paul talks of us giving generously within our means (2 Corinthians). What does this mean in terms not just of money but time, commitment and even faith and trust?

Notes

HE IS HERE TO SHOW US HOW POWERFUL GOD'S LOVE IS

SO WHAT DOES THIS REVEAL ABOUT JESUS AND HIS MISSION?

HE MUST BE GOD'S SON

HE SPEAKS WITH AUTHORITY BIGGER THAN DEATH

TO TEACH HIS DISCIPLES WHO HE IS

HE FEELS SORRY FOR PEOPLE WHO ARE SAD

HE HAS COME TO BRING US ALL TO LIFE

JESUS

HIS MISSION

RAISING THE DEAD

IS JAIRUS' DAUGHTER THE ONLY PERSON JESUS RAISED FROM THE DEAD?

No – Jesus brought a young man to life because he felt sorry for the widowed mother. And when Lazarus, Jesus' friend, had died, Jesus raised him after he'd been dead for four days.

IT JUST SEEMS SO IMPOSSIBLE TO BRING ANYONE TO LIFE AGAIN – UNLESS THEY WEREN'T COMPLETELY DEAD YET.

Well, don't forget we're looking at the Lord of life here – not just anybody. Actually Jesus tells the girl's parents that she is only sleeping but they just laugh at him.

THE GIRL WAS MADE COMPLETELY BETTER, WASN'T SHE?

Oh yes – and she was very hungry!

BECKY
* JAIRUS' 12-YEAR-OLD DAUGHTER
* DANGEROUSLY ILL
* JESUS BROUGHT HER BACK TO LIFE

JAIRUS
* WORRIED AND SAD
* HAS FAITH THAT JESUS CAN HELP
* LOVES HIS YOUNG DAUGHTER
* CONVINCED SHE IS REALLY DEAD

JAMES, JOHN AND PETER
* THE 3 DISCIPLES ALLOWED TO WATCH
* WITH JESUS EVERY DAY
* WONDERING WHO JESUS CAN BE

BE STILL, FOR THE POWER OF THE LORD IS MOVING IN THIS PLACE;
HE COMES TO CLEANSE AND HEAL,
TO MINISTER HIS GRACE.
NO WORK TOO HARD FOR HIM,
IN FAITH RECEIVE FROM HIM.
BE STILL, FOR THE POWER OF THE LORD IS MOVING IN THIS PLACE.

(Taken from the song *Be still, for the presence* by David J. Evans, © 1986 Kingsway's Thankyou Music)

1. READ THE ACCOUNT IN MARK 5
2. TAKE ON ONE OF THE ROLES
3. EACH CHARACTER TELLS THE STORY FROM THEIR OWN POINT OF VIEW

PROPER 9

Sunday between 3 and 9 July inclusive

Thought for the day

If we are not ready to listen to the truth, we will not hear it.

Readings

2 Samuel 5:1-5, 9-10 or Ezekiel 2:1-5
Psalm 48 or Psalm 123
2 Corinthians 12:2-10
Mark 6:1-13

Aim

To look at how the message is to be preached, whether people want to listen or not.

Starter

Play 'pick-up-sticks', either with a commercial set, or by tipping a pile of cutlery on to the table and taking it in turns to lift off one item at a time very carefully, so as not to wobble the rest.

Teaching

That was a bit how it feels to be talking about our faith to someone who is determined not to believe a word of what we're saying! We have to go very carefully and sensitively, looking out for where those people are coming from, so we can talk into their questions and help them understand. Today we are reading about the way the people in Jesus' home town reacted to him. Read Mark 6:1-6 and look out for why they rejected him.

However, there were huge numbers of people living in the area who needed to be told the good news, so this is how Jesus decided to reach those people. Read Mark 6:7-13 and look out for the instructions Jesus gave his disciples as he sent them off. They are to do with travelling light, living simply and involving the community.

Now read the passage from Ezekiel, where the prophet is told to tell out God's words, even though he knows there will be many who refuse to listen. Talk together about our own lives and the people we know. How are they to be told about the God who made them and longs for them to live freely in his forgiving love, instead of living just for material things and personal comfort?

Pray for one another in the group about particular situations that come up in the conversation, and particular people they want to help hear God's message.

Praying

Lord, help me to listen properly
so that I hear your voice, your will for me,
your comfort and your challenges.
And help me to speak out your good news
so others may hear your voice, your will for them,
your comfort and your challenges.
Amen.

Activities

On the sheet there is a short script to draw their attention to different ways of not listening, and some help with training ourselves into a habit of daily prayer. They are also encouraged to look at how the call to pass on God's message affects them.

Discussion starters

1. How genuinely receptive are we to God's word? Do we mark out 'no-go' areas where God is concerned?

2. How might our gut reactions alert us to God trying to tell us something important, which we don't really want to hear?

Notes

DRAMA SPOT

THE BASIC SCRIPT

Can I talk to you for a minute? It's just that . . . well, I've been noticing how you're treating Cliff lately, and it bothers me. You look at him as if he's a slug, and snap his head off whenever you speak.

RESPONSE Ⓐ

Fidget, shuffle, avoid eye contact, look at your watch. Interrupt to say your bus is due.

RESPONSE Ⓑ

Angry, accuse them of always getting at you and always criticising. Refuse to accept what they say.

RESPONSE Ⓒ

Change the subject and talk over the other person till they give up.

CHOOSE A RESPONSE AND TRY IT OUT WHILE SOMEONE DOES THE BASIC SCRIPT.

THERE ARE LOTS OF WAYS WE MANAGE NOT TO LISTEN!

I DIDN'T WANT TO HEAR THAT!

IT DOESN'T FEEL NICE TO HAVE WRONG THINGS POINTED OUT — EVEN IF YOU KNOW THEY'RE TRUE.

I agree. We usually try our best not to really hear what's being said! Herodias didn't want to hear what John the Baptist said.

DO YOU THINK SHE REALLY KNEW SHE WAS IN THE WRONG?

Probably.

DO YOU THINK JOHN THE BAPTIST KNEW HE'D BE UNPOPULAR FOR SPEAKING OUT?

Probably! But it didn't stop him, did it?

I BAPTISE YOU IN THE NAME OF THE FATHER...

AM I CALLED TO FIGHT AGAINST EVIL?

FIGHT VALIANTLY AS A DISCIPLE OF CHRIST AGAINST SIN, THE WORLD AND THE DEVIL!

LORD, HELP ME TO LISTEN PROPERLY SO THAT I HEAR YOUR VOICE, YOUR WILL FOR ME, YOUR COMFORT AND YOUR CHALLENGES. HELP ME TO SPEAK OUT YOUR GOOD NEWS SO OTHERS MAY HEAR YOUR VOICE, YOUR WILL FOR THEM, YOUR COMFORT AND YOUR CHALLENGES. — AMEN —

SUNDAY	MONDAY	TUESDAY	WEDNESDAY	THURSDAY	FRIDAY	SATURDAY	SUNDAY
Make a regular time for prayer each day	Try lighting a 'prayer candle' as you pray	Use the sections of the Lord's Prayer like headings of prayer	Keep a prayer note book to pray for different people each day of the week	Spread out the newspaper and 'pray' the news	Have photos of those you pray for	Include – Penitence, Praise, Thanks, Intercession, Adoration	Check with yourself each Sunday to keep up the habit

GET IN TRAINING GET THE DAILY PRAYER HABIT

SOME HINTS AND IDEAS ...

PROPER 10

Sunday between 10 and 16 July inclusive

Thought for the day

Those who speak out God's will are bound to be vulnerable to rejection and abuse.

Readings

2 Samuel 6:1-5, 12b-19 or Amos 7:7-15
Psalm 24 or Psalm 85:8-13
Ephesians 1:3-14
Mark 6:14-29

Aim

To look at why speaking out God's truth is often dangerous.

Starter

Tie a length of string across the room at just above head height and provide two different coloured balloons. Split the group either side of the string, each with a balloon. Both sides aim to get their balloon to touch the floor on the other side, while preventing the other balloon from coming to land on their own side.

Teaching

Draw attention to the way we all did our best to hit that approaching balloon back where it came from. We do just the same in arguments. If someone says something about us that we don't want to hear, we hit it back as fast as we can. Today we are reading about the way prophets are treated when they go on speaking out God's words which people don't want to hear.

Read either the 2 Samuel or the Amos passage, noticing in both how faithfulness to God is despised and rejected. Then read today's Gospel, where John the Baptist is hated and eventually put to death because the words of God which he insists on speaking out are uncomfortable for Herodias to hear. Suppose instead of shutting her ears to what John was saying, she and Herod had listened. What might have happened?

When we shut our ears to hearing what God wants us to know, we shut out all kinds of possible good in our lives, and open up all kinds of possibilities of evil.

If you have time, look at Ephesians 1:3-14, or at least verses 4-7. It is Christ's life in us, and the forgiveness of our sins that makes it possible for us to live God's way – we can't do it on our own without

his grace. Also it's important that they understand God's love for us doesn't depend on how well we behave. Getting our lives upright in God's sight is our response to the love God lavishes on us, not the way to earn his love.

Praying

Refiner's fire,
my heart's one desire is to be holy,
set apart for you, Lord.
I choose to be holy,
set apart for you, my Master,
ready to do your will.

(Taken from the song *Purify my heart* by Brian Doerksen
© 1990 Mercy/Vineyard Publishing/Music Services/CopyCare)

Activities

On the sheet there are some quotations from people imprisoned for continuing to live God's way even when it is dangerous, and they are looking at what they can do to support those in prison at the moment for their faith, or other Christians locally who could do with some encouragement.

Discussion starters

1. How ready are we to speak out God's truth and God's values when we know they will make us unpopular?

2. How can we best support and encourage the young people as they live and work in environments often openly hostile to God?

Notes

Sheila Cassidy is a doctor. She was imprisoned and tortured for treating a wounded person whom the ruling party disapproved of. She is a Christian.

· SHEILA CASSIDY
· DOCTOR IN CHILE

"I think it was during this time of waiting that I was conscious of praying. I remember little except that I prayed for strength to withstand the pain and for courage to die with dignity if that was to be my fate. Most of all I remember a curious feeling of sharing in Christ's passion. Sick and numb with pain and fear, spread-eagled so vulnerably on the bunk, it came to me that this was perhaps a little how it had been for him one Friday morning so many years before."

From *Audacity to believe*
© 1992 Darton, Longman & Todd Ltd

Michele Guinness is Jewish. She became a Christian and her family at first disowned her.

"My fingers trembled on the dial, then somehow found the right numbers. It was ringing.

Oh, let them be out, please!

'Hello! Oh, it's you, darling. How are things?'

'Mum, I'm going to be baptised.'

The silence seemed interminable.

'I said . . .'

'I know what you said.' The voice was cold and hard. 'Never come home again. You're no longer our daughter.'

Click! The line was dead."

From *Child of the Covenant*
© 1985 Hodder & Stoughton Ltd

· MICHELE GUINNESS

BEING A CHRISTIAN CAN BE DANGEROUS

HOW CAN IT BE DANGEROUS TO LIVE LOVINGLY AND DO WHAT'S RIGHT?
Because you may find people tease you or are nasty to you for doing that, and for going to church and for praying.

SUPPOSE I JUST PRETEND I'M NOT A CHRISTIAN?
You can do that. But if, as a Christian, you see things happening which you know are offensive to God, you might feel you have to speak out.

BUT DIDN'T JESUS PROMISE TO GIVE US THE WORDS TO SAY WHEN THAT HAPPENS? Yes! And he will keep that promise. Even if you are insulted, God will keep you and protect you from evil whatever happens.

Gonville f-Beytagh was Dean of the Anglican Cathedral in Johannesburg, South Africa. At that time, concern for black Africans was seen as treason, and he was imprisoned, in solitary confinement.

"To have nothing to do is a devastating, destroying thing; I learnt that through being unemployed in the slump in the 1930s when I wasn't wanted by anybody. I learnt it too in solitary confinement. On one day I crawled round the floor of my cell and found some bristles from a broom. I spent a longish time weaving them into a tiny cross, and that was good because I had found something to do."

From *A glimpse of glory*
© 1986 Darton, Longman & Todd Ltd

· GONVILLE FFRENCH-BEYTAGH

REFINER'S FIRE,
MY HEART'S ONE DESIRE
IS TO BE HOLY,
SET APART FOR YOU, LORD.
I CHOOSE TO BE HOLY,
SET APART FOR YOU,
MY MASTER,
READY TO DO YOUR WILL.

(From the song *Purify my heart* by Brian Doerksen, © 1990 Mercy/Vineyard Publishing/Music Services/CopyCare)

HOW CAN WE SUPPORT THOSE IMPRISONED AT THE MOMENT FOR THEIR FAITH?

IDEAS

PROPER 11

Sunday between 17 and 23 July inclusive

Thought for the day

Like a good shepherd, Jesus sees the needs of his people and always responds with love.

Readings

2 Samuel 7:1-14a or Jeremiah 23:1-6
Psalm 89:20-37 or Psalm 23
Ephesians 2:11-22
Mark 6:30-34, 53-56

Aim

To see how Jesus' ministry as leader and shepherd fulfilled the prophecies.

Starter

What's my line? Take it in turns to mime a job while the others try to work out what job it is.

Teaching

Begin by reading what God thought of the job being done by the leaders of his people during the time of Jeremiah, not long before they were taken off into Babylon as exiles. On the sheet there is space to jot down the reasons why God is going to punish these irresponsible leaders. Also draw attention to the love God has for his people as he talks of a future leader who will take proper care of them. That would be quite a job, and only one person could do it.

Look next at the Gospel to see Jesus in action, and the passage from Ephesians. Jot down what everyone notices about his ministry, as if you are compiling a job description. (For example: on call 24 hours a day; no guaranteed regular holiday. Accommodation and food variable according to availability and others' hospitality; salary £00.00. Highly demanding but highly rewarding work.)

Praying

The Lord is my shepherd,
I have everything I need.
He gives me rest in green pastures.
He leads me to calm water.
He gives me new strength.
True to his name
he leads me on paths that are right.

(From Psalm 23)

Activities

There is space on the sheet to record the needs of God's people, suffering under bad leaders, and the practical loving shepherding that Jesus provides, reflecting the Father's love. They are encouraged to imagine what such a ministry would feel like as a disciple, as Jesus himself, and as someone among the crowds.

Discussion starters

1. Jesus tried to ensure that his disciples had times of rest and spiritual refreshment. Do we follow that example in our church community?

2. Why were the crowds going out of their way to flock to Jesus?

Notes

WHAT'S JEREMIAH TELLING THE PEOPLE?

THE LEADERS OF GOD'S PEOPLE ARE ...

BUT ONE DAY ...

B·C

WANTED:
LEADER TO SHEPHERD GOD'S PEOPLE PROPERLY. WILLING TO GIVE UP EVERYTHING. NO MONEY. NO SECURITY. VITAL WORK.
QUALIFICATIONS:

JESUS SHEPHERDS GOD'S PEOPLE

HOW DID JESUS KNOW WHAT TO DO?

He kept in close touch with his Father in heaven, praying every day – lots. Also, he could see the needs of the people. So he met their needs.

IT MUST HAVE BEEN SO AMAZING TO BE THERE WHEN JESUS WAS AT WORK.

Yes – no wonder the crowds flocked to hear and see him. They could tell he loved them.

WHAT JOB IS JESUS DOING?

THE LORD IS MY SHEPHERD,
I HAVE EVERYTHING I NEED.
HE GIVES ME REST IN GREEN PASTURES.
HE LEADS ME TO CALM WATER.
HE GIVES ME NEW STRENGTH.
TRUE TO HIS NAME
HE LEADS ME ON PATHS
THAT ARE RIGHT.
(– FROM PSALM 23 –)

HOW WOULD IT HAVE FELT TO BE THERE AS ...

...ONE OF THE DISCIPLES?

...AS JESUS HIMSELF?

...AS SOMEONE AMONG THE CROWDS?

PROPER 12

Sunday between 24 and 30 July inclusive

Thought for the day

Out of God's riches, a great crowd is fed and satisfied from a small offering of food.

Readings

2 Samuel 11:1-15 or 2 Kings 4:42-44
Psalm 14 or Psalm 145:10-18
Ephesians 3:14-21
John 6:1-21

Aim

To see how this feeding prefigures the feeding of the Last Supper and Holy Communion.

Starter

Bread tasting. Bring a selection of breads from different parts of the world, together with an atlas or world map. Find where each bread comes from and sample it. All over the world bread of some kind is basic food.

Teaching

Begin by reading the passage from 2 Kings, where Elisha feeds a hundred people with a gift of bread. Notice the generosity (in offering the bread) and Elisha's careful listening to God's will, and his wholehearted obedience to it.

Now look at the feeding of the five thousand in John's Gospel. Draw attention to the timing – it's about Passover time. (Another meal, just before the escape from slavery.) Look at what Jesus does with the food – he accepts the gift, gives thanks to God for it, breaks it in pieces and gives it out to the people to feed them when they are hungry.

Link this with what Jesus started at the Passover meal he shared with his disciples before his death, and which goes on happening in all our churches right through the centuries and the generations, all over the world. That is quite a crowd being fed! And we are part of that same blessing, breaking and giving out which has been going on for about two thousand years. It's a record-breaking meal.

Finally read from Ephesians 3. All that feeding, with daily food for our bodies and daily spiritual food as well, is an outpouring of God's extraordinary love which is higher, deeper, wider and greater than we can ever imagine.

Praying

(From Ephesians 3, a prayer to pray for each other)

I pray that Christ will live in your hearts
because of your faith.
I pray that your life will be strong in love
and built on love.
And I pray that you and all God's holy people
will have the power to understand
the greatness of Christ's love –
how wide and high, long and deep that love is.

Activities

On the sheet there are pictures of Christians from different times in history and different countries, all taking part in God's feeding programme. The actions of Jesus are linked with what happens in church at the Eucharist.

Discussion starters

1. When faced with our next problem which looks insurmountable, how can today's Gospel help us do things God's way?

2. Why do you think John mentions that the feeding of the five thousand takes place at the time of the Jewish Passover? What other meal would Jesus preside over at Passover?

Notes

THE FEEDING GOES ON AND ON... 5 LOAVES AND 2 FISHES WASN'T MUCH TO START WITH, WAS IT?

Not in itself, no. But it was one person's willingness to be generous, and God can do a lot with that.

SO IF I OFFERED MY LIFE, EVEN THOUGH I'M ONLY ONE PERSON AND ONLY ME, COULD GOD USE THAT GIFT IN THE SAME WAY?

Yes! And when you get to heaven you'll see just how many people were blessed through your giving!

PROPER 13

Sunday between 31 July and 6 August inclusive

Thought for the day

Jesus is the Bread of Life who satisfies our hunger and sustains us on our journey to heaven.

Readings

2 Samuel 11:26-12:13a or Exodus 16:2-4, 9-15
Psalm 51:1-12 or Psalm 78:23-29
Ephesians 4:1-16
John 6:24-35

Aim

To explore the significance of Jesus describing himself as the Bread of Life.

Starter

This person . . . Sit in a circle, and take it in turns to describe someone (who may be famous, or someone everyone knows), not by looks but by different things they do or have done. Whoever guesses the identity can have the next go.

Teaching

We managed to work out who those people were without knowing anything about their appearance. We know hardly anything about Jesus' appearance, but we can tell a great deal about him by what he said and did. Today we're going to look at one of the ways Jesus described himself.

Read today's Gospel, writing 'I am the Bread of Life' on a large sheet as it comes up. Talk about what Jesus might have meant by this. (Look at what bread does for our physical bodies and then look at how Jesus does this in a spiritual way – feeding, satisfying hunger, providing essentials for growth and health and energy, and so on.)

Now look back to the Exodus passage and Psalm 78, referred to in the Gospel, so that they can see the connection and the background to the way Jesus was thinking. Who did the people think had provided them with manna in the desert? (Look at Jesus' reply in John 6:32.) Remembering how the crowd had just recently been miraculously fed by Jesus, talk about what they might have meant in verse 30 of John 6. What does it mean to 'believe in the one God sent'? (Verse 29)

Point out that we all walk straight past things we're not prepared or expecting to see, and some of the people couldn't believe that Jesus could be anywhere near as holy as Moses, the holy figure from the past. They didn't realise that Moses had been pointing towards this moment, and that they happened to be alive at the very time God's Son came to the earth.

Finally look at Ephesians, where we are shown how this risen life, nourished by the Bread of Life, works out in practice. Notice anything they recognise from their own experience of Christians, and anything which they feel our own community is falling short on.

Praying

Lord Jesus Christ,
I would come to you,
live my life for you,
Son of God.
All your commands I know are true,
your many gifts will make me new,
into my life your power breaks through,
living Lord.

(Taken from the song Lord Jesus Christ *by Patrick Appleford © 1960 Josef Weinberger)*

Activities

On the sheet today's teaching is reinforced with space to record the qualities of bread which help us understand about the nature of Jesus. They are also helped to see the links between God's feeding of his people in the desert and our feeding as a travelling people.

Discussion starters

1. Do we realise our need of Jesus' feeding, or think of it more as an optional extra?

2. How can our God-given work in life just be to believe in Jesus? (What difference does that belief make to everything else we do?)

Notes

CIRCLE THE ONES YOU THINK!

IT KEEPS US ALIVE
WHOLEMEAL
IT HELPS YOU ENJOY OTHER FLAVOURS
IT'S OUR NATURAL FOOD
WE NEED IT FOR FOOD
VISIBLE NOURISHMENT
IT GIVES US STRENGTH AND ENERGY
IT TASTES GOOD
PITTABREAD
WHITE
RYE
IT DOES US GOOD
CORNBREAD
NAAN BREAD
GRANARY
CRUSTY

OUR · DAILY · BREAD · GIVE · US

JESUS IS THE BREAD OF LIFE

WHY DID HE CALL HIMSELF BREAD?

Well, think about what bread is like, and what it does.

OK – YOU EAT IT WHEN YOU'RE HUNGRY AND IT DOES YOU GOOD. YOU NEED TO EAT IT EVERY DAY TO KEEP STRONG AND HEALTHY. AND IT TASTES GOOD!

Very good! So when Jesus calls himself 'Bread of Life' it means that when we're spiritually hungry he feeds us and keeps us spiritually strong and healthy.

WHAT IS IT ABOUT BREAD THAT MADE JESUS SAY I AM THE BREAD OF LIFE...

JOHN 6:35

JOHN 6:27

EGYPT

A TRAVELLING PEOPLE

EXODUS 16: 11–12

EPHESIANS 4:16

LORD JESUS CHRIST,
I WOULD COME TO YOU,
LIVE MY LIFE FOR YOU,
SON OF GOD.
ALL YOUR COMMANDS
I KNOW ARE TRUE,
YOUR MANY GIFTS WILL
MAKE ME NEW,
INTO MY LIFE YOUR POWER
BREAKS THROUGH, LIVING LORD.

(Taken from the song *Lord Jesus Christ* by Patrick Appleford, © 1960 Josef Weinberger)

A TRAVELLING PEOPLE – US!

PROPER 14

Thought for the day

Just as bread is the visible form of life-giving nourishment, so Jesus is the visible form of God's life-giving love.

Readings

2 Samuel 18:5-9, 15, 31-33 or 1 Kings 19:4-8
Psalm 130 or Psalm 34:1-8
Ephesians 4:25-5:2
John 6:35, 41-51

Aim

To explore ways in which we can read God's signs.

Starter

Use the road signs on page 128 and write up the 'spiritual' meanings separately. Fix them all around the walls. Send everyone round to match them up.

Teaching

Read the passage from 1 Kings 19, where Elijah is provided with the rest, food and drink he needs to continue in God's calling. Elijah is exhausted and depressed as he walks into the desert, and he recognises that God is providing for him in the shady tree, the much-needed sleep, the bread and the water. He understands these things as signs of God's love, because he is already used to being attentive to God and expecting God to communicate with him. Too often we don't notice God's care of us through the ordinary things of life, but actually every meal, every shower when we're hot and sticky, every clean bed we collapse into, every patch of shade . . . all of these ordinary, everyday things are signs to us of God's love for us, and we just take it all for granted, unless we've recently had to do without such luxuries! God's practical provision enables us to do the work he calls us into.

Jesus' commission is to be our Saviour, acting out God's total love in words and actions throughout his life. Sometimes this must have been uplifting and thrilling, as great crowds began to understand how God was reaching out to them. But at other times the message had to continue to be proclaimed in the face of hostility, as in today's Gospel. (Read that now.)

Jesus is claiming a very special relationship with God, which has been backed up by signs and miracles of many different kinds. The stage is set for the religious leaders to hail him as the true Messiah, for whom they have been waiting for generations, and towards whom Moses and the prophets had carefully directed their hearers and readers.

But the religious leaders cannot and do not read the signs.

Now read the passage from Ephesians, which gives some excellent advice for keeping ourselves ready to notice God's signs. It is all to do with regularly cleaning up after ourselves, recognising that we need to check our position and direction with God, several times in each day. Knowing God's love for us has the effect of making us actually want to keep coming back like this – we do it not out of fear or a burdensome duty, but out of love and gratitude, knowing that so much more of the positives can happen, and life feels right when we are right with God.

Praying

A man that looks on glass,
on it may stay his eye;
or, if he chooses, through it pass,
and thus the heavens espy.
Lord, in all the outward things,
let me see you and learn from you.
Amen.

Activities

On the sheet there are various signs to read, and they are encouraged to read the signs of the natural world which tell us of God's nature. They also look at some of the everyday signs of God's practical caring, linking Elijah's feeding with Jesus coming to us as 'Bread from heaven'.

Discussion starters

1. Are we aware of when we are listening to learn and understand, and when we are not? Do we really want to hear whatever God says to us?

2. Are we taking Jesus up on his offer of feeding, and relying on it for dear life, or do we tend to glance at the Bread of Life but commit ourselves to spiritual junk food – or spiritual starvation?

Notes

READING GOD'S SIGNS

WHAT SORT OF SIGNS DOES GOD GIVE US TO READ? Well, there's the universe – everything we know and live in, everything we see and hear, and all the invisible things, too.

WHAT DO THEY ALL MEAN? That depends on what God wants to show us. One day you might see heavy rain which makes you realise how God showers and soaks us with his love. Another day the rain might remind us of how God shares the sadness and suffering of our world.

HOW DO I KNOW IT'S GOD SPEAKING AND NOT JUST MY OWN THOUGHTS? Good question. God does talk to us through our thoughts but he is always true to his nature. So if the thoughts are selfish, unloving or dishonest, they are not of God. If they match up with God's nature, they probably are God speaking to you.

WHAT DO THESE SIGNS MEAN ???

GOD'S FAITHFULNESS AND RELIABILITY

GOD'S POWER

HOW CAN THINGS IN OUR WORLD SHOW US...

GOD'S ORDER AND ATTENTION TO DETAIL

GOD'S IMAGINATION AND HUMOUR

O LORD, LET ME DIE!

WHAT ORDINARY THINGS DID GOD USE TO HELP ELIJAH GO ON?

"I AM THE LIVING BREAD"

"A MAN THAT LOOKS ON GLASS, ON IT MAY STAY HIS EYE; OR IF HE CHOOSES, THROUGH IT PASS AND THUS THE HEAVENS ESPY." LORD, IN ALL THE OUTWARD THINGS, LET ME SEE YOU AND LEARN FROM YOU.
—AMEN—

WHAT ORDINARY WAYS DOES GOD USE TO SHOW US HIS LOVING CARE?

Proper 15

Sunday between 14 and 20 August inclusive

Thought for the day

God's wisdom may appear foolishness without the God-given grace to understand.

Readings

1 Kings 2:10-12; 3:3-14 or Proverbs 9:1-6
Psalm 111 or Psalm 34:9-14
Ephesians 5:15-20
John 6:51-58

Aim

To see how God's wisdom is sometimes seen as foolishness.

Starter

Sing one of those silly songs with actions, such as 'Did you ever see a zombie come to tea? Take a look at me – a zombie you will see.' With each verse an extra action is added: marching with feet, right arm up and down, left arm up and down, nod head, blink.

Teaching

Now we have all made ourselves look ridiculous! Today we are going to look at how God's wisdom is often seen as complete foolishness. Perhaps they have already been made to feel foolish for believing in God and talking to him. It is never a nice experience, and can set us wondering why we bother with God if it's going to make some people laugh at us and think we're stupid. (Of course, God is there whether we bother with him or not, so it won't make God disappear if we deny him. Nor will it help those who are doing the scoffing. But we do need to support one another with our prayers, and to know that Jesus received the same scorn from his contemporaries.)

Read the passage from Proverbs, telling them also about the lady Folly, in contrast to Wisdom. At first sight Folly can look like a good idea, appealing to our instincts and cravings, rather like much of the media does today. Only after people have made their choice is it clear that this leads to death, whereas the path of Wisdom leads to life-giving nourishment and fulfilment.

Go on to read the passage from Ephesians, discussing what 'living wisely' means for us. Draw out the need to be actively involved in goodness, rather than just not doing anyone any harm.

Now look at today's Gospel, where the religious leaders are finding it impossible to see Jesus' words as wisdom, but only as foolishness and blasphemy. What stops them seeing the truth of Jesus' words? (Look at their expectations of the Messiah, their attention to precise detail at the expense of the wider vision, and their status as learned, respected leaders in the community.)

Praying

Be thou my wisdom, be thou my true word,
I ever with thee and thou with me, Lord;
thou my great Father, and I thy true heir;
thou in me dwelling, and I in thy care.

(From a song translated from the Irish
by Mary Byrne and Eleanor Hull
© Copyright Control)

Activities

On the sheet they are helped to look at some of the things which those who cannot accept God find foolishness, and to see how they are in fact wisdom, though contrasting to the world's values. They are also encouraged to see how they can live wisely, making the most of every opportunity to do good and fight against evil.

Discussion starters

1. What is the difference between being clever, learned and knowledgeable, and being wise?

2. Why do learned and clever people often find it harder to understand God's wisdom? Should this affect the way our children are 'taught'?

Notes

WISDOM v. FOOLISHNESS

HOW CAN WISDOM BE FOOLISHNESS, OR THE OTHER WAY ROUND FOR THAT MATTER?

It all depends where you're standing. Some people would consider it wise to go walking in the mountains all day, others would think it a foolish waste of energy.

SO IS IT THE SAME WITH GOD'S WISDOM?

Yes, only more so. It might seem wise to spoil yourself and insist on your own way, but living against God's Law of love is foolishness in the long term.

WHAT IS WISDOM, THEN?

Seeking out God's will for us and our world, and living in harmony with the One who designed us.

THE SON OF GOD BEING A CARPENTER FROM NAZARETH

THE GREAT AND AWESOME G-O-D WALKING ABOUT AMONG ORDINARY PEOPLE

THE MESSIAH MAKING FRIENDS WITH THE RIFF RAFF OF SOCIETY

THE MESSIAH SHOWING UP THE RELIGIOUS TEACHERS OF THE SACRED LAW AS HYPOCRITES

IT'S NOT GOD'S WISDOM — IT'S TOTAL FOOLISHNESS!

PUT A SQUARE ROUND GOD'S WISDOM / WORLD'S FOOLISHNESS

PUT A CIRCLE ROUND THE WORLD'S IDEA OF WISDOM

ALWAYS LOOK AFTER NUMBER 1 AT ALL COSTS.

PUT YOURSELF OUT FOR OTHERS, LOVING THEM.

AIM TO IMPRESS OTHER PEOPLE SO THEY RESPECT YOU AND VALUE YOU.

WHAT YOU LOOK LIKE AND BUY IS EXTREMELY IMPORTANT.

TO BE BEAUTIFUL IN GOD'S EYES HAS NOTHING TO DO WITH HOW YOU LOOK.

STOP WORRYING ABOUT WHAT IMPRESSES PEOPLE AND LEARN TO SEEK GOD'S WILL.

BE THOU MY WISDOM,
BE THOU MY TRUE WORD,
I EVER WITH THEE AND
THOU WITH ME, LORD;
THOU MY GREAT FATHER
AND I THY TRUE HEIR;
THOU IN ME DWELLING
AND I IN THY CARE.

(From a song translated from the Irish by Mary Byrne and Eleanor Hull, © Copyright Control)

PROPER 16

Sunday between 21 and 27 August inclusive

Thought for the day

'To whom else could we go? You alone have the words of eternal life.'

Readings

1 Kings 8:(1, 6, 10-11) 22-30, 41-43 or
Joshua 24:1-2a, 14-18
Psalm 84 or Psalm 34:15-22
Ephesians 6:10-20
John 6:56-69

Aim

To explore why the split happened at this point.

Starter

Why? (This is a variation on *Call my bluff.*) Split the group into two teams and give each some kind of bell or other noise item. Whoever is first with the right choice wins the round. Here are some ideas to start you off.

1. Why did the campanologist climb the stairs? (a) Because he was camping at the top of a mountain; (b) because he was campaigning in high-rise flats; (c) because the bells he was ringing were in a tower.

2. Why was the kleptomaniac arrested? (a) Because she was a compulsive clog dancer; (b) because she was a compulsive thief; (c) because she was a compulsive stalker.

3. Why did Jeremiah not have sore armpits? (a) Because his friends padded them with rags; (b) because he never shaved them; (c) because he used Oil of Ulay every day.

4. Why did the student need his portfolio? (a) Because he was going to sea; (b) because he wanted to choose some wine to celebrate passing his exams; (c) because his artwork was carried in it.

Teaching

Why do we do the things we do? Often there isn't just one reason but lots of little reasons and events that come together. (Why, for instance, is each person here today?) Today we are looking at people making important decisions, and why they made them.

Read the passage from Joshua, with the people's choice based on their personal experience of Yahweh's care and their trust in what Joshua, their leader, advises. Then read the Gospel for today.

Why did they find what Jesus was saying so hard that it made them decide to walk no more with him? Share ideas about this, and help them to see that in making those statements, Jesus was saying that he was the Holy One of God, and this was a very hard thing to accept, especially for Jewish people who thought of God as so awesome that they never even allowed themselves to say his name. The thought of the transcendent God walking among them in sandals was mind blowing, so they came to the conclusion that Jesus must either have gone OTT or was a liar.

But if he really was telling the truth – and all the evidence pointed to that – then God's Son was actually standing with them, breathing the same air.

Following such a controversial belief may well be dangerous. Read Ephesians to find out how God helps us here.

Praying

Yes, Lord, I believe that you are the Christ,
the Son of God who has come into the world.
I have decided to follow you,
for you alone have the words of eternal life.

Activities

On the sheet there are different reasons for believing that the world is flat/round. They can use these to see how we come to conclusions which others would challenge unless they have plenty of evidence. They then compare Peter and the disciples' reasons for concluding that Jesus is the Holy One of God, compared with those who turn away.

Discussion starters

1. What do we actually believe Jesus to be, and how does this affect our life?

2. Why do you think Jesus made no attempt to persuade those who turned away to return?

Notes

1. I can walk along on it

2. The sky looks like a big upturned bowl over me – the sky comes down to the flat ground all around me

3. People I respect have told me

I BELIEVE THE WORLD IS FLAT BECAUSE ....

I BELIEVE THE WORLD IS ROUND BECAUSE ....

1. Ships disappear over the horizon

2. I've seen pictures taken of the world from space

3. People I respect have told me

THE WORDS OF ETERNAL LIFE

IF JESUS HAD THE WORDS OF ETERNAL LIFE HE MUST BE MORE THAN JUST A HUMAN, LOCKED IN TIME LIKE THE REST OF US.

Exactly. Peter and the others had recognised that Jesus was the promised Holy One of God.

HOW DID THEY KNOW?

They'd spent time with him and seen how he behaved and what he did. All those healings, all the teaching, all the love. And it fitted in.

FITTED IN WITH WHAT?

With everything written in the books of the Law, the prophecies and the psalms.

HOW DO WE COME TO CONCLUSIONS?

GUESSING

SCIENTIFIC PROOF

WISHFUL THINKING

PERSONAL EXPERIENCE

WHAT THOSE WE RESPECT HAVE TOLD US

WHAT WE'VE ACTUALLY SEEN

IF THE FACTS FIT THE THEORY

WHAT THOSE WE ADMIRE BELIEVE

SO WHY DID PETER AND THE DISCIPLES COME TO THIS CONCLUSION?

... WHILE THE RELIGIOUS TEACHERS CAME TO THIS CONCLUSION?

JOHN 6:69

JOHN 8:48

YES, LORD, I BELIEVE THAT YOU ARE THE CHRIST, THE SON OF GOD WHO HAS COME INTO THE WORLD. I HAVE DECIDED TO FOLLOW YOU, FOR YOU ALONE HAVE THE WORDS OF ETERNAL LIFE.

PROPER 17

Thought for the day

We need to be careful never to replace the timeless commands of God with man-made traditions.

Readings

Song of Solomon 2:8-13 or Deuteronomy 4:1-2, 6-9
Psalm 45:1-2, 6-9 or Psalm 15
James 1:17-27
Mark 7:1-8, 14-15, 21-23

Aim

To look at the benefits and dangers of tradition in the Church.

Starter

On separate pieces of card write down various traditions, which they sort into 'Very important', 'Non-essential' and 'Chuck'. Here are some ideas: Christmas pudding; a white wedding; wearing black at funerals; school uniform; dinner before dessert; milk poured in before the tea; standing for the national anthem; salt and vinegar with chips; homework; wearing best clothes to church; ladies first.

Teaching

Lots of our traditions are so much part of life that we only notice them when we travel abroad and find they're not there. Sometimes we take it for granted that anything we're used to doing must be right. Today we're going to look at that and question it, as Jesus did.

First read the passage from Deuteronomy, reminding them of the basic principles of the Law – Love God and love one another. Make a list of the advantages of having traditions in place to help keep the Law. Use the sheet to see how the extra 'fence' of rules and regulations became part of the tradition, from the best of motives, but having the effect of shifting priorities in people's minds.

Now read the Gospel passage from Mark 7, picking out the dangers and disadvantages of having intricately worked-out traditional customs. What had happened to the way the people thought of religious duty?

Finally read from Ephesians, where we are taken back to basics, in line with what Jesus taught. How is true religion described? Talk over the traditions of our own church, looking at what is obviously very precious and important, and what seems to them to be rather in line with some of the religious teachers' rules and regulations.

Praying

Lord, I want to show my love and thanks
in the way I live my life.
I want everything I think, say and do
to be in line with your Law of love.
Lord, help me to be more concerned
with the state of my soul before you,
than with my efforts to impress other people.
Amen.

Activities

There is space on the sheet to work out quantities of time, energy and money spent on various things in life, in order to assess what our life is actually displaying. And they are helped to see how the build-up of regulations grew out of a genuine desire to keep the Law faithfully.

Discussion starters

1. What might Jesus take offence at in the Church today which claims to be the Body of Christ?

2. Do we still accept Jesus' teaching that the 'uncleanness' which so often leads to sin comes from the inside of people, or is responsibility for sin being replaced by genetics and other circumstances beyond our control?

Notes

HOW MUCH SPENT ON EDUCATION, HEALTH AND DEFENCE IN U.K. 1998

Defence £22.5b
Health £45.0b
Education £38.9b

ONE YEAR

BACK TO BASICS –

WHAT BASICS DO YOU MEAN?

The commandments of God – love God and love one another.

IF THE JEWISH PEOPLE ALREADY HAD THE BASIC LAW, WHY DID JESUS HAVE TO TAKE THEM BACK TO IT?

Jesus was challenging them to look at how all their little extras had obscured the law of love.

I WONDER IF THE CHRISTIAN CHURCH HAS DONE THE SAME THING, WITH ALL ITS TRADITIONS?

I wonder. What do you think?

HOW MUCH OF YOUR TIME DO YOU SPEND ON SLEEPING, WORKING LEISURE, HELPING OTHERS ...

ONE DAY

SO WHAT DOES YOUR LIFE ACTUALLY SAY ABOUT YOU?

HOW THE EXTRAS GREW AND GREW ...

HOW MUCH OF YOUR MONEY DO YOU SPEND ON YOURSELF, OTHER PEOPLE, GIVING TO CHARITY ...

Don't do this on the Holy Day

Don't do that on the Holy Day

YOUR "INCOME"

I AM RICH!

THAT'S SO SPECIAL. LET'S PROTECT IT WITH A FENCE OF RULES!

LOVE GOD

Only walk this much on a Sabbath

Since God is undivided, don't put different things together for eating or wearing

LORD, I WANT TO SHOW MY LOVE AND THANKS IN THE WAY I LIVE MY LIFE.
I WANT EVERYTHING I THINK, SAY AND DO TO BE IN LINE WITH YOUR LAW OF LOVE.
LORD, HELP ME TO BE MORE CONCERNED WITH THE STATE OF MY SOUL BEFORE YOU THAN WITH MY EFFORTS TO IMPRESS OTHER PEOPLE.
– AMEN –

OH NO, HOW TERRIBLE. JESUS IS HEALING ON THE SABBATH. HOW CAN HE IF HE LOVES GOD?

PROPER 18

Sunday between 4 and 10 September inclusive

Thought for the day

Jesus comes fulfilling the hope of healing to wholeness; he shows that mercy has triumphed over judgement.

Readings

Proverbs 22:1-2, 8-9, 22-23 or Isaiah 35:4-7a
Psalm 125 or Psalm 146
James 2:1-10 (11-13) 14-17
Mark 7:24-37

Aim

To look at the Christian attitude to prejudice and discrimination.

Starter

Size, shape, colour. All work together (or in smaller groups) on the puzzle shown below. No adjoining shapes can have more than one thing in common.

Teaching

Being able to discriminate between things is an important skill which we need to have. But often our society is full of discrimination of the wrong sort, selecting those who are acceptable and those who are not; those we respect and those we can despise. There's also lots of prejudice (the word means judging before you've even met) and today's readings help us discover what Jesus' views are.

First read the prophecy from Isaiah, noticing the wide-ranging healing it describes, with nothing and no one excluded or shut off by physical disabilities.

Then read the passage from James, looking out for some advice for us about discrimination and prejudice. As one of the proverbs says, the thing that rich and poor have in common is that God made them both! This passage challenges our attitudes as individuals, as the Church and as members of a nation. Draw attention to mercy triumphing over judgement.

Now read the Gospel for today. There are two stories of people who were shut off, or excluded, before being welcomed in – one because she is a total 'outsider' and the other through the silence of hearing loss. Notice how the prophecy is being fulfilled without Jesus forcing things to happen, but simply responding to needs as they present themselves. Mercy has triumphed over judgement.

Praying

Father we pray for all who are cut off
from the world of sight and hearing,
and for those who just feel
cut off and left out.
Jesus didn't leave anyone out.
Teach us to live that way too.
Amen.

Activities

On the sheet there are various hot potatoes to look at in the Church and in society concerning discrimination and prejudice, and they are helped to look at these in the light of the Gospel. They are drawing up a few guidelines for challenging the rest of us as well, and these could perhaps be printed in the magazine or the local newspaper.

Discussion starters

1. Can we appreciate mercy unless we first appreciate the judgement we deserve?

2. How do we stand, as Church and as a nation, in relation to issues of discrimination and prejudice?

MERCY HAS TRIUMPHED OVER JUDGEMENT

MERCY MEANS LETTING YOU OFF—RIGHT?
Right. It's not excusing you, and pretending you weren't wrong. It's knowing you were in the wrong and letting you off anyway.

LIKE BEING LET OFF A BAD DEBT?
Yes. God gives us forgiveness for free, and we're to do the same, forgiving other people instead of harbouring grudges.

SOMETIMES PEOPLE HARBOUR GRUDGES FOR NO REASON AT ALL, DON'T THEY?
Sadly, yes. Our world is full of people who are shut out by prejudice and discrimination.

WHAT CAN WE DO AS CHRISTIANS?
Aim to live free of prejudice, respecting every other human being as a child of God.

PROPER 19

Sunday between 11 and 17 September inclusive

Thought for the day

Loving obedience to God is shown by Jesus to be a quality rich in courage and wisdom, a quality to be highly respected.

Readings

Proverbs 1:20-33 or Isaiah 50:4-9a
Psalm 19 or Wisdom of Solomon 7:26-8:1 or
Psalm 116:1-9
James 3:1-12
Mark 8:27-38

Aim

To explore the value and importance of Jesus' loving obedience, and its implications for us as his followers.

Starter

Collect some snails and stage a snail race down a premarked sheet of A4 paper.

Teaching

However much we shouted encouragement at our snails, they weren't able to be particularly obedient either to us, or the ruled lines marking their lanes. They still have no idea of what they were supposed to be doing. Today we are going to look at what obedience really is.

Begin by reading the passage from Isaiah 50, describing God's obedient Servant, willing to go along with God's guidance even in the face of violent opposition. Who does it sound like? For us, living after Jesus' coming, the passage points very significantly to Jesus, describing the kind of loving obedience he showed during all his life and particularly in his trial and crucifixion. This kind of obedience came from the way Jesus was always so close to his Father – at one with him, so that God's will was also Jesus' will.

Now look at today's Gospel from Mark 8. Jesus is making it plain that part of being the Christ is the necessity to go through the suffering foretold by the prophets. That loving obedience is all part of Jesus' identity as the Messiah, or holy, anointed One of God. And Jesus goes further; it's also part of being someone who claims to be one of Christ's followers, like us. If we mean what we say, it will involve a daily willingness to walk the way of the cross (verse 34).

Have the words of the Lord's Prayer available, and draw their attention to the way the first section of the prayer is placing ourselves in that loving obedience, whenever we say, 'Let your kingdom come; let your will be done on earth as it is in heaven.' Do we realise what we are saying here? We need to do that conscious placing of ourselves in obedience to God every single time we say those words – and say them at least morning, afternoon and evening every day.

If you have time, look at the passage from James, thinking about the damage that can be done by not keeping our tongues in obedience to God's rule of love.

Praying

Our Father in heaven, hallowed be your name.
Your kingdom come.
Your will be done on earth as it is in heaven.

Activities

On the sheet there is an example of how the tongue can be a powerful instrument for spreading both trouble and good. Examples of Jesus' loving obedience are used to help us in our obedience, and they are encouraged to work out what obedience involves.

Discussion starters

1. Has the time come to take another look at obedience and see if we've grown up enough to consider it a Godly quality worth developing?

2. Why does Jesus say that following him is bound to involve taking up our cross as he did?

Notes

LOVING OBEDIENCE

BUT I DON'T LOVE OBEDIENCE – I HATE DOING WHAT I'M TOLD!

Me too! But I didn't say 'love obedience' – I put an 'ing' on it!

OH-RIGHT. SO WHAT'S THE DIFFERENCE?

Well, there's a big difference between grumpily obeying because you'll get grounded if you don't, and doing what your parents say because you love them.

LIKE GETTING IN WHEN THEY TOLD YOU TO SO THEY DON'T WORRY ABOUT YOU?

Exactly. Jesus didn't always LIKE what he had to do, any more than we do. But he did it anyway, out of love for God his Father and love for us.

PHILIPPIANS 2:5-8

YOUR ATTITUDE SHOULD BE ...

OUR FATHER IN HEAVEN, HALLOWED BE YOUR NAME. YOUR KINGDOM COME. YOUR WILL BE DONE ON EARTH AS IT IS IN HEAVEN.

Proper 20

Sunday between 18 and 24 September inclusive

Thought for the day

The truly great in God's eyes are those who are prepared to be last of all and servant of all.

Readings

Proverbs 31:10-31 or Wisdom of Solomon 1:16-2:1,
12-22 or Jeremiah 11:18-20
Psalm 1 or Psalm 54
James 3:13-4:3, 7-8a
Mark 9:30-37

Aim

To understand Jesus' teaching about greatness and servanthood.

Starter

Have a number of pictures of famous people from newspapers and magazines cut out and stuck around the room, numbered. Give out sheets of paper. Everyone goes round writing down the names of those pictured. The one with most right gets to wear a posh hat to show how clever they are.

Teaching

All the people in those pictures were famous, for all sorts of reasons. They were all 'the greatest' in their particular area. Now read today's Gospel, where the disciples have been arguing about which of them should be the greatest. Why were they ashamed to admit to Jesus what they had been talking about? Why might their argument have disturbed Jesus? (He knew that they were going to be the leaders of the Church, and here they were behaving like pagan leaders, full of boasting and jealousy.) Notice how Jesus both explains and shows them, with the little child, what he means. Children were vulnerable, and with no status at all, so to accept Jesus by accepting them suggests that he is prepared to think of himself on a level with what most people would consider the very lowest of the low. (How do we choose our friends? Would we feel embarrassed to be seen with some people because our other friends despise them?)

Now read the passage from James. There are more arguments here, and James is helping his hearers understand where all this strife comes from. That makes it easier to sort out, provided we genuinely want it sorted. Sometimes people enjoy having their battles and moans. Look at the sound advice James gives. He helps us see that Satan fools us into thinking he's big and powerful, but if we really stand our ground and fix our feet in what we know is right and good, Satan's power trickles out of him, and he slinks away. This is a very useful image for when we find ourselves being tempted, and it always works.

Praying

The world wants the wealth to live in state,
but you show us a new way to be great:
like a servant you came
and if we do the same
we'll be turning the world upside down.

(Taken from the song *O Lord, all the world* by Patrick Appleford © 1965 Josef Weinberger)

Activities

There is a short sketch to look at the reasons for arguments, linked with the James reading, and some information about status so that they can better grasp what Jesus is saying in today's Gospel. There are some different life ambitions to consider.

Discussion starters

1. How much does the Church look as if it is based on the principle of the greatest being the last and the servant of all? Does anything need changing?

2. Look at examples of arguments and strife – personally, locally and internationally – and see if they do come from what Jesus and James suggest.

Notes

– Can I have a go now?
– No.
– Oh, come on, you've been on it for hours.
– Yeah, I know. It's mine, remember?
– Well, you're mean, hogging it all the time.
  I only want a little go.
– Shut up and go away. This level's really hard and I
  need to concentrate.
– Well, I hope the hard drive crashes, then. And don't
  expect to borrow my bike tomorrow.

WHAT CAUSES ARGUMENTS?

King   We need more land.

Queen   We could take some from the country
next door, dearest.

King   Mmm, yes, good idea. I've been
meaning to get my own back on
them for polluting our rivers.

Queen   Shall I call the chief army commander
for you then, dear?

King   Yes – we'll build up forces on our side
to frighten them, and when they shoot
at us we'll blast in and flatten them!

Queen   More tea, dear?

LOWEST OF THE LOW

WHO IS ?

That depends what age you live in,
and which culture. But it's those who
have no rights, no influence and very
little money, and most people have
little respect for them.

WHO WAS THAT IN JESUS' TIME ?

Slaves, servants, women and children,
plus the social outcasts.

**SO WHEN JESUS USED A YOUNG CHILD
AS AN EXAMPLE IT WASN'T FOR
THE "AH, HOW CUTE" VALUE ?**

Exactly. He was showing them
someone considered lacking all
power and status.

**AND WE'RE TO THINK OF OURSELVES
AS SERVING EVEN THEM !**

You've got it.

SELFISHNESS   ENVY   HOLDING GRUDGES

JEALOUSY   GREED   THINKING WE DESERVE MORE THAN OTHERS

THINKING WE ARE MORE IMPORTANT THAN OTHERS   WANTING WHAT ISN'T OURS

HOW CAN WE GET TO A WIN/WIN SITUATION ?

THE WORLD WANTS THE WEALTH TO LIVE IN STATE,
BUT YOU SHOW US A NEW WAY TO BE GREAT:
LIKE A SERVANT YOU CAME
AND IF WE DO THE SAME
WE'LL BE TURNING THE WORLD UPSIDE DOWN.

(Taken from the song *O Lord, all the world* by Patrick Appleford
© 1965 Josef Weinberger)

PROPER 21

Thought for the day

Don't let your body lead you into sin and risk exchanging eternal life for eternal punishment.

Readings

Esther 7:1-6, 9-10; 9:20-22
or Numbers 11:4-6, 10-16, 24-29
Psalm 124 or Psalm 19:7-14
James 5:13-20
Mark 9:38-50

Aim

To look at the importance of being prepared for temptation.

Starter

Press flour into a pudding basin with a coin somewhere inside and carefully upend it so you have a pudding-shape of flour. People take turns at slicing the 'pudding' without making it collapse, and without dislodging the coin. Continue until one of those things happens, and the one who was cutting a slice at the time has to clear it all away. But they can keep the coin!

Teaching

Today we're looking at resisting temptation. If we're not well prepared for it, we're more likely to find our good intentions collapsing in a cloud of dust, like our flour pudding. We're taking temptation seriously because Jesus did. He was tempted very severely just after his Baptism, during his ministry and in the garden of Gethsemane, just before he was arrested, and he urgently warned his disciples to watch and pray so that they wouldn't give way to temptation. They didn't realise how important it was, and ended up scattering, and leaving Jesus when he most needed them.

Begin by reading today's Gospel, from Mark 9, picking up on how seriously Jesus is wanting us to take this teaching. He uses strong, violent examples to make us think, and to help us recognise what a real battle it can be to resist evil; it isn't something to treat casually because the effects are so lasting and so damaging, both to ourselves and others, not just in this life but after death as well. Jesus is suggesting that we take strong action to turn our backs on temptation before it drags us into sin. As soon as a sin looks attractive to us – tempting – our danger lights should start flashing and that's when we

need to take action. If we don't, the temptation will just get stronger, and harder to resist.

Temptation is well worth resisting, because sin is long-term destructive. Our job as Christians is to be preservers of eternal life, like salt preserves food.

Now look at the passage from Numbers, seeing how temptation works on the people, and the trouble it causes. Also notice the link between Joshua's protest and the disciples' protest in Mark 9:38, and the similarity between Moses' and Jesus' replies.

Praying

The dearest idol I have known,
whatever that idol be,
help me to tear it from thy throne
and worship only thee.

Activities

On the sheet the passage from James draws attention to faithful prayer and its effectiveness. There is also a diagram showing how temptation works and how we can short circuit it in God's strength.

Discussion starters

1. Do we believe that prayer is truly effective or not? If not, what may be blocking the power?

2. Jesus is very serious about not leading the vulnerable into sin. What can we actively do in our society as those concerned for the eternal wellbeing of souls?

Notes

PROPER 22

Sunday between 2 and 8 October inclusive

Thought for the day

Human beings are made responsible for the care of creation but are subject to God in all aspects of their lives.

Readings

Job 1:1; 2:1-10 or Genesis 2:18-24
Psalm 26 or Psalm 8
Hebrews 1:1-4; 2:5-12
Mark 10:2-16

Aim

To explore responsibility and faithfulness in caring for our world and in our relationships.

Starter

Play consequences. Each section is written and passed on around the circle, before the disjointed stories are read out. (Girl) met (boy) at (place). He said to her (. . .), she said to him (. . .), and the consequence was (. . .).

Teaching

Practically every book, film and soap is about people and their relationships, falling in and out of love, marrying, divorcing, quarrelling, making up and messing up. Today we are going to look at what the Bible teaches us about faithfulness and responsibility, both with one another and with the natural world.

Begin by reading the passage from Genesis, looking at the way humankind, in the person of Adam, is placed in a position of responsibility, to care for the world and look after it. Notice how life-long partnership is seen as God's way of providing us with companionship and help, as we work under God's rule for the good of the world.

Now read today's Gospel, where Jesus is teaching his disciples about divorce. He reminds them of the Genesis passage we have just read, reinforcing that God's way of faithfulness and responsibility in a lifelong relationship is good and rewarding. What does that mean for us as Christians, living in a time of easy divorce? It means we're going to need really serious thought and lots of prayer as we go about choosing a partner with whom we're expecting to have to spend the rest of our life, through the difficult times and broken nights, and financial worries and growing children, as well as the high spots and romantic bliss!

Praying

Lord, for ourselves;
in living power remake us –
self on the cross
and Christ upon the throne,
past put behind us,
for the future take us,
Lord of our lives,
to live for Christ alone.

(Taken from the song *Lord, for the years*
by Timothy Dudley-Smith
© Timothy Dudley-Smith)

Activities

On the sheet there is a questionnaire to help them look at choosing a marriage partner for life, as a basis for discussion about this issue. Other callings in life are also explored. There is also space given to the responsible care of our universe, with examples of good and bad stewardship.

Discussion starters

1. Should our aim in life for ourselves and our children be happiness or goodness? How will this affect our attitude to life's troubles and hardships?

2. How can we ensure that we take Jesus' teaching on marriage seriously, while recognising that some marriages cause such pain and damage?

Notes

THE SINGLE LIFE

WHAT ABOUT OTHER CALLINGS ???

LIFE IN A COMMUNE

LIVING AS A MONK OR A NUN

UNITED NATIONS AIMS FOR AGREED POLICY ON FORESTATION

CUSTOMERS DEMAND FAIRLY TRADED COFFEE

FEWER AND FEWER PEOPLE TRAVEL BY PUBLIC TRANSPORT

INDUSTRIAL POLLUTION POISONS MANY VILLAGES IN INDIA

RESPONSIBILITY AND FAITHFULNESS

THAT SOUNDS LIKE HARD WORK.
True – but it's rewarding hard work. When we're being responsible and faithful in our relationships and in looking after our world, it feels 'right' for us.

WE CAN'T DO IT ALONE, THOUGH, CAN WE? No – it's a shared thing and is much easier if everyone joins in. But if others don't, that doesn't let us off.

DO YOU THINK GOD SOMETIMES GIVES US PARTICULAR JOBS OF RESPONSIBILITY TO DO?
I'm certain of it. And when he does that, he also gives us the courage and strength to do them.

CHOOSING A MARRIAGE PARTNER

Number in order of importance

Someone you can be best friends with	
Someone who's rich	
Someone who shares your faith in God	
Someone you find physically attractive	
Someone you can be honest with	
Someone whose parents are nice	
Someone who does what you tell them	
Someone who shares your interests	
Someone who wants children	
Someone who respects you	

LORD, FOR OURSELVES;
IN LIVING POWER REMAKE US –
SELF ON THE CROSS
AND CHRIST UPON THE THRONE,
PAST PUT BEHIND US,
FOR THE FUTURE TAKE US:
LORD OF OUR LIVES,
TO LIVE FOR CHRIST ALONE.

(Taken from the song *Lord, for the years* by Timothy Dudley-Smith, © Timothy Dudley-Smith)

PROPER 23

Thought for the day

The word of God is living and active, piercing right to the heart; only with God is it possible to be saved.

Readings

Job 23:1-9, 16-17 or Amos 5:6-7, 10-15
Psalm 22:1-15 or Psalm 90:12-17
Hebrews 4:12-16
Mark 10:17-31

Aim

To ask the young man's question.

Starter

Have two people turning a long skipping rope. The others have to try getting through the turning rope without getting entangled.

Teaching

Have the words of the young man written down and explain that this was a question put to Jesus by a young man. Talk over what they would say to the young man if they were asked the question.

Now read today's Gospel, with different people taking the various parts. How does Jesus' response compare with ours? Notice how he doesn't answer directly, but addresses what is going on in the man's mind as well as what he actually asks.

Next read the passage from Amos or Job, looking at the importance of seeking God and how doing so actually affects the way we live. God is found through the seeking. Go back to the Gospel where the disciples ask how anyone at all can be saved, and see how Jesus tells them that this is impossible for us to do for ourselves; we need God for it, and then it becomes possible.

Finally read the passage from Hebrews, and think about what effect Jesus' words had on the young man, both immediately and possibly after he had calmed down a bit. The word of God is just as challenging to us, and just as effective, if we listen to it.

Praying

All that I dream, all that I pray,
all that I'll ever make I give to you today.
Take and sanctify these gifts
for your honour, Lord,

Knowing that I love and serve you
is enough reward.
All that I am, all that I do,
all that I'll ever have I offer now to you.

(Taken from the song *All that I am* by Sebastian Temple © 1967 OCP Publications, USA)

Activities

The sheet reinforces the teaching in the Gospel, with them taking a look at the things in their own lives that would be hard to give up, and a look at Christians who can witness to how they have gained through sacrificing things for Jesus.

Discussion starters

1. How can we help one another through the dark times when God does not seem to be answering us or making himself known?

2. What makes it so incredibly worthwhile to follow Jesus, in spite of the difficulties?

Notes

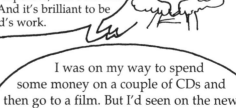

PROPER 24

Sunday between 16 and 22 October inclusive

Thought for the day

Even the Son of Man himself came not to be served but to serve, and to give his life as a ransom for many.

Readings

Job 38:1-7 (34-41) or Isaiah 53:4-12
Psalm 104:1-9, 24, 35c or Psalm 91:9-16
Hebrews 5:1-10
Mark 10:35-45

Aim

To explore the concept of Jesus being a Servant King.

Starter

Human sculpture. One person is the sculptor, and the others are his medium to work with. He explains where he wants each person to be and how to arrange their body, until the whole group has turned into a sculpture. Then someone else can be the sculptor.

Teaching

Begin by reading either the Job or the Isaiah passage. In the passage from Job, God is seen in all his majesty and glory, and Job is humbled to realise he has no right to question the creator of all things. In Isaiah, we see God's chosen One as a servant, suffering, humbled and broken, laying aside his majesty for the good of the world.

Go on to the reading from Hebrews, explaining that the Jewish priests were appointed to represent the people and offer sacrifices to God on their behalf. The writer points out that, owing to their own sinfulness, they needed to include themselves in this. Jesus, like a high priest, is also appointed by God, and becomes the perfect sacrifice to take away the sins of the whole world. (Link this with the Agnus Dei – 'Lamb of God, you take away the sins of the world' – which they meet in the Communion service.)

Now read Mark 10:35-45, seeing how Jesus' calling to be the suffering servant ties in with the prophecies, and jars against what James and John are wanting. Like Jesus, we are called to the servant role.

Praying

My song is love unknown,
my Saviour's love for me,
love to the loveless shown,
that they may lovely be.
O who am I, that for my sake,
my Lord should take frail flesh and die?

Activities

On the sheet they are helped to explore the concept of the suffering servant, which Jesus recognised as his route to save the world. There are also some examples of leadership to consider in the light of Jesus' teaching.

Discussion starters

1. Even if we grasp the idea of being servants, how can we stop ourselves striving to be the most important and highly honoured servants of Christ?

2. Is Jesus' model for leadership practical? Do we practise it in the Church and in our lives?

Notes

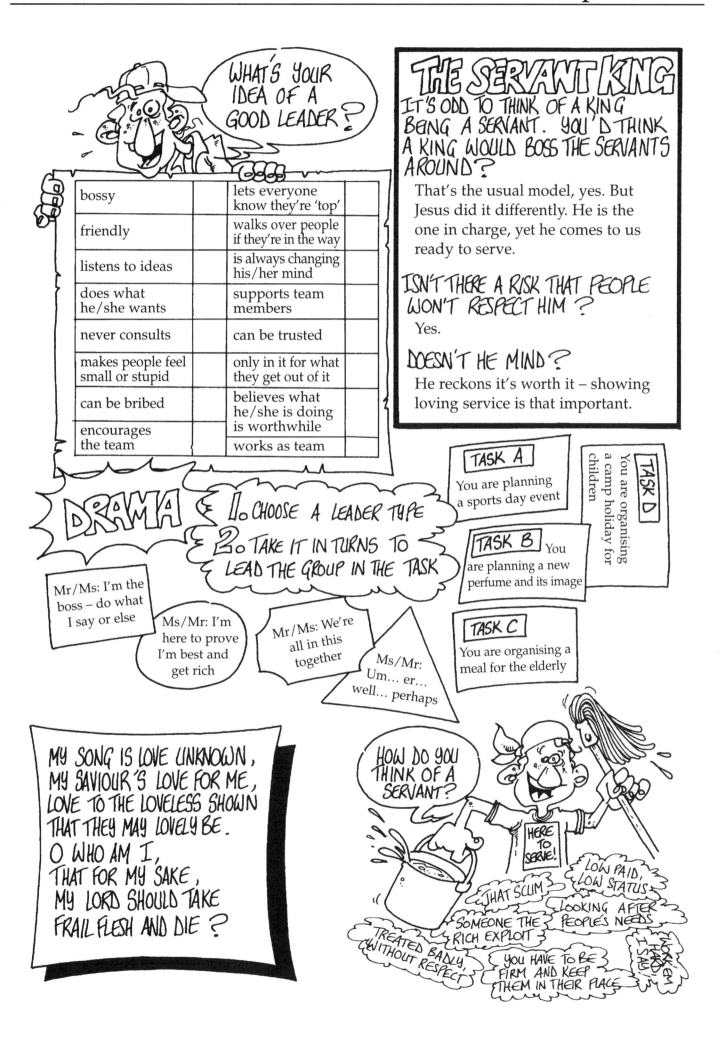

WHAT'S YOUR IDEA OF A GOOD LEADER?

bossy	lets everyone know they're 'top'	
friendly	walks over people if they're in the way	
listens to ideas	is always changing his/her mind	
does what he/she wants	supports team members	
never consults	can be trusted	
makes people feel small or stupid	only in it for what they get out of it	
can be bribed	believes what he/she is doing is worthwhile	
encourages the team	works as team	

THE SERVANT KING

IT'S ODD TO THINK OF A KING BEING A SERVANT. YOU'D THINK A KING WOULD BOSS THE SERVANTS AROUND?

That's the usual model, yes. But Jesus did it differently. He is the one in charge, yet he comes to us ready to serve.

ISN'T THERE A RISK THAT PEOPLE WON'T RESPECT HIM?

Yes.

DOESN'T HE MIND?

He reckons it's worth it – showing loving service is that important.

DRAMA

1. CHOOSE A LEADER TYPE
2. TAKE IT IN TURNS TO LEAD THE GROUP IN THE TASK

Mr/Ms: I'm the boss – do what I say or else

Ms/Mr: I'm here to prove I'm best and get rich

Mr/Ms: We're all in this together

Ms/Mr: Um… er… well… perhaps

TASK A You are planning a sports day event

TASK B You are planning a new perfume and its image

TASK C You are organising a meal for the elderly

TASK D You are organising a camp holiday for children

MY SONG IS LOVE UNKNOWN,
MY SAVIOUR'S LOVE FOR ME,
LOVE TO THE LOVELESS SHOWN
THAT THEY MAY LOVELY BE.
O WHO AM I,
THAT FOR MY SAKE,
MY LORD SHOULD TAKE
FRAIL FLESH AND DIE?

HOW DO YOU THINK OF A SERVANT?

HERE TO SERVE!

THAT SCUM
LOW PAID, LOW STATUS
LOOKING AFTER PEOPLE'S NEEDS
SOMEONE THE RICH EXPLOIT
TREATED BADLY WITHOUT RESPECT
YOU HAVE TO BE FIRM AND KEEP THEM IN THEIR PLACE

PROPER 25

Sunday between 23 and 29 October inclusive

Thought for the day

In Jesus, God gathers his scattered people and opens their eyes to see.

Readings

Job 42:1-6, 10-17 or Jeremiah 31:7-9
Psalm 34:1-8, 19-22 or Psalm 126
Hebrews 7:23-28
Mark 10:46-52

Aim

To see how, in Jesus, God gathers his scattered people back and opens their eyes to see.

Starter

Make a tape of assorted sounds. They have to work out what the sounds are.

Teaching

With the aid of biblical maps, show how the split north kingdom of Israel was overcome by the Assyrians and the people taken into exile. Soon after that Assyria was attacked and conquered by the Babylonians.

Jeremiah lived in the south kingdom of Judah just after this, when Judah was caught in the middle between the Egyptians and the Babylonians. Before long Jerusalem itself would be captured and all except the poorest people of Judah deported to Babylon. Not happy times. Jeremiah was trying hard to warn the people that they really needed to unite under God's law, committing themselves to him completely.

Now read the passage from Jeremiah, with its picture of people returning to God with all their hearts. As we know, the people didn't listen, and they were taken into exile, eventually returning to a ruined city. But the hope developed that one day, a 'son of king David' would be a special king, filled with God's power, who would lead his people back to God's ways.

Next look at the Gospel, with different people reading the various parts. Here we have the blind man calling out to Jesus as 'son of David'. In Jesus that great hope has become a real person, walking around Jericho and the other cities, towns and villages, bringing people back to God and healing them. Today we have yet another example of such healing.

Praying

Praise, my soul, the King of heaven!
To his feet thy tribute bring;
ransomed, healed, restored, forgiven,
who like me his praise should sing?
Praise him! Praise him!
Praise him! Praise him!
Praise the everlasting King!

Activities

On the sheet there are examples of people returning after deportation, and they are encouraged to imagine the feelings at such a time. There are also examples of those who have returned to God after a long time of self-imposed exile, and how they feel. They can make a collage of returning with joy, using pictures, words and colours to express the sense of Psalm 126.

Discussion starters

1. In what way do Jesus' disciples help (or hinder) Bartimaeus from coming to Jesus for healing?

2. How do we help (or hinder) people from coming to Jesus?

Notes

GOD GATHERS HIS SCATTERED PEOPLE

DOES THAT MEAN PEOPLE IN EXILE?

Not just exile from their country. It's also talking about those who have wandered away from God.

LIKE NOT BELIEVING IN GOD ANYMORE?

Yes – and saying they believe but living selfishly.

I'M GLAD GOD WANTS TO GATHER THEM ALL UP. YOU'D THINK HE MIGHT GIVE UP ON US.

Yes. But our loving God never gives up on anyone.

COMING BACK HOME FROM EXILE

IT WAS A REAL EYE-OPENER, I CAN TELL YOU!

I CAN SEE IT ALL, NOW...

PUFF PUFF PUFF

IF ONLY I'D SEEN HOW UPSET HE WAS!

OH, NOW I SEE!

THERE ARE MANY WAYS OF BEING GIVEN YOUR SIGHT.

WHAT DO THESE REALLY MEAN?

HOW HAS GOD HELPED YOU "SEE" BETTER?

SOLDIERS BACK FROM WAR

REFUGEES BACK TO PICK UP THEIR LIVES AGAIN

PRAISE, MY SOUL, THE KING OF HEAVEN!
TO HIS FEET THY TRIBUTE BRING;
RANSOMED, HEALED, RESTORED, FORGIVEN,
WHO LIKE ME HIS PRAISE SHOULD SING?
PRAISE HIM! PRAISE HIM!
PRAISE HIM! PRAISE HIM!
PRAISE THE EVERLASTING KING!

I THINK I WOULD FEEL ...

ALL SAINTS' DAY

Sunday between 30 October and 5 November inclusive

Thought for the day

Great is the rejoicing in heaven among the saints of God as they worship their Lord in glory.

Readings

Wisdom 3:1-9 or Isaiah 25:6-9
Psalm 24:1-6
Revelation 21:1-6a
John 11:32-44

Aim

To look at the nature of sainthood.

Starter

Give one person a painting of heaven as painted by an artist (a print such as you find on some Christmas cards, where heaven is visible above the stable; or in an art book). Without the others seeing the picture, the person describes it to them in detail, and they imagine it. Then everyone is shown the actual picture. How is it like they imagined, and how is it completely different?

Teaching

Today we are celebrating all the lives well lived and shining with God's love. Anyone who has continued faithfully on their journey through life, close to God and ready to work with him, will be among those living for ever in the joy of heaven. The reading from Wisdom looks forward to this promise (read this passage), and Psalm 24 celebrates those who are eligible. (What does the psalmist mean by having clean hands and a pure heart?)

Now read the passage from Revelation, which picks up on both the Wisdom and Isaiah readings, and the Gospels which have many references to the righteous living and rejoicing in heaven. Jesus talked about it as a definite. The writer is describing the welcome into heaven in picture language.

In today's Gospel we have a very different picture. We are not in heaven but just outside a village near Jerusalem. Jesus calls his dead friend Lazarus not into heaven but back into the temporary and dangerous world we all know. One day he will have to go through the dying again. But the reading speaks about Jesus being the Lord of life, and gives us some idea of the voice which calls faithful servants from the darkness of death into the everlasting light of heaven.

Praying

Here might I stay and sing,
no story so divine;
never was love, dear King,
never was grief like thine.
This is my friend in whose sweet praise
I all my days could gladly spend.

Activities

There are some marks of sainthood for them to consider and some examples of saints, both ancient and modern. They are encouraged to think about the image of gold being refined and purified in relation to lives being lived.

Discussion starters

1. If your life was in a book of saints, what would you like it to say about you?

2. Which saint do you particularly admire and why?

Notes

GOLD REFINING IN PROGRESS

GOLD IS MELTED

LUMP OF RAW GOLD

VERY HOT FIRE

FIRE BURNS OFF THE IMPURITIES

PURIFIED GOLD IS POURED INTO A MOULD

ONE BAR OF PURE GOLD!

HOW IS THAT LIKE OUR LIVES AS CHRISTIANS?

SAINTS

WOULD I RECOGNISE A SAINT IF I MET ONE?

Probably. You'd keep thinking, 'That's how Jesus would be'.

I KNOW SOME PEOPLE WHO GO TO CHURCH LOADS, BUT TO BE HONEST, THEY DON'T STRIKE ME AS BEING MUCH LIKE JESUS.

Going to church lots doesn't automatically make you a saint. It's living closely with Jesus that changes you.

EVEN ME?

Yes, even you!

MEET A FEW SAINTS...

Bernard joined the Cistercian order at the age of 22, along with 31 of his friends. They joined the abbey at Citeaux, saving it from closure. Bernard later became the abbot and helped the expansion of the Cistercian order – at his death there were 400 houses in Europe. He led the failed second crusade but is better remembered for his contributions to monastic life. (died 1153)

SAINT BERNARD

Monica had family problems – her husband was violent and unfaithful, and her son, Augustine of Hippo, initially refused to follow Christianity. But Monica hung on to God through all her difficulties. Her husband became a Christian a year before his death, and Augustine travelled to Rome and was baptised there. (died 387)

SAINT MONICA

HERE MIGHT I STAY AND SING, NO STORY SO DIVINE; NEVER WAS LOVE, DEAR KING, NEVER WAS GRIEF LIKE THINE. THIS IS MY FRIEND IN WHOSE SWEET PRAISE I ALL MY DAYS COULD GLADLY SPEND.

Patrick's experiences as a slave in a foreign land led him to rely deeply on God. In later life he returned to the land of his captivity as a missionary. He showed a real aptitude for stamping out paganism by adopting new meanings for old festivals so that all the people could understand. He is the patron saint of Ireland.

SAINT PATRICK

(died c. 460)

FOURTH SUNDAY BEFORE ADVENT

*Sunday between 30 October and 5 November inclusive**

* For use if the Feast of All Saints was celebrated on 1 November and alternative propers are needed

Thought for the day

To love the living God with heart, soul and strength, and to love our neighbour as ourselves means far more than any sacrificial offerings.

Readings

Deuteronomy 6:1-9
Psalm 119:1-8
Hebrews 9:11-14
Mark 12:28-34

Aim

To see the priority of loving God.

Starter

Everyone makes their own favourite design paper plane, adjusting it for optimum flying. See whose can fly best and furthest.

Teaching

With the paper planes, the basic design was important, and also aligning and balancing, adjusting the shape to stop it crashing. Today we are looking at getting our lives aligned and adjusted in keeping with the best design of all.

Read the passage from Deuteronomy, explaining that the people were just about to cross over into the Promised Land. What was their 'design for living' going to be? How were they going to make sure it never got forgotten?

Tell them about the way the priests, on behalf of the people, regularly sacrificed animals, sprinkling the people with the animals' blood and offering the burnt sacrifice to God as a way of cleansing the people from sin. Show them some pictures of this. Now look at Hebrews 9:11-14, seeing how Jesus, being both the priest figure and the sacrificial victim (the Lamb of God), was able to do the cleansing of the people's sin once and for all. The people would understand about being 'made clean' by the blood of animal sacrifices, so it made sense to them that the blood of Jesus, poured out for us on the cross, was able to cleanse us of sin completely.

Now explain how some of that offering of sacrifices had become empty ritual over the years, with the people doing all the actions, and having lots of rules about correct procedures, but living lives which were not in a loving relationship with God. The scribe in today's Gospel was one of those who recognised this and worried about what really was important.

Read the Gospel, so they can see how Jesus cut through all the accumulated complications, right to the very heart of the matter – loving the one true God with our whole heart and soul and mind and strength.

Praying

Be thou my vision, O Lord of my heart,
naught be all else to me save that thou art;
thou my best thought in the day and the night,
waking or sleeping, thy presence my light.

(From a song translated from the Irish
by Mary Byrne and Eleanor Hull
© Copyright Control)

Activities

On the sheet there is a picture of the sacrifices being offered, together with the scribe's words in verse 33 of Mark 12. They are encouraged to explore the difference between correct practices and a loving relationship. They also learn about the Shema, and the effect of Jesus reciting it in the context of his teaching.

Discussion starters

1. Jesus answers the seeking scribe's question not with argument but with a statement of faith. What can we learn from this?

2. What is our priority in life?

Notes

THIRD SUNDAY BEFORE ADVENT

Sunday between 6 and 12 November inclusive

Thought for the day

When we are called we need to respond with obedience so that many may be brought to repentance.

Readings

Jonah 3:1-5, 10
Psalm 62:5-12
Hebrews 9:24-28
Mark 1:14-20

Aim

To look at vocation and our response.

Starter

Give out a circled job advertisement in a newspaper, and prepare three or four simple profiles to give the applicants, including such facts as age, qualifications and experience. The rest of the group are the panel interviewing them for the job, and they decide which one to appoint.

Teaching

When God calls people for particular jobs, he already knows all about them, and knows they will be perfectly suited to the work he is calling them to. (That's why it's such a sensible idea to consult God when we are thinking about jobs we might do.) But when God calls, it doesn't always look like what we were hoping to do.

Read the passage from Jonah, reminding them of what had happened the first time God wanted Jonah to call the citizens of Nineveh to repentance. In today's passage we find Jonah being obedient to his call, and the people are also obedient to their calling; they decide to reject their evil ways and turn back to God. God knew that Jonah was the right person for the job, but he could only use him if Jonah willingly agreed. All kinds of good doesn't get done because the people God wants to call aren't listening.

Now look at the calling of the first disciples in today's Gospel. These four people hear the call and respond to it straightaway. Something in Jesus makes them sure that this wild and crazy idea of following a wandering preacher is a good one, if unusual and unexpected. They can feel how important it is, even though they don't yet know exactly why.

When God calls us, he doesn't lay all the details out straightaway. He just lodges the conviction in us that we have to follow him in a particular direction, and as we start to follow, the next bit of the job becomes clearer. He never forces or pressurises us, though if, like Jonah, we start haring off in the other direction, he'll wait to get our attention again and then quietly repeat the same call. If we agree to follow, he'll set off and expect us to keep up with him. The fishermen were probably surprised it happened to be they who were called; we shouldn't be too surprised if we find God calling us!

Praying

For God alone my soul in silence waits;
truly my hope is in him.
He alone is my rock and my salvation,
my stronghold, so that I shall not be shaken.
In God is my safety and my honour;
God is my strong rock and my refuge.

(From Psalm 62)

Activities

On the sheet they are helped to see different ways God calls people, and to explore some of the reasons for listening or refusing to listen. They look at vocation in its broadest sense, both as long-term work and for particular tasks.

Discussion starters

1. Are there occasions when we sense God's call and direction but fail to run with it in case we are mistaken?

2. What makes people able to understand and respond to a call to repentance and what hinders them?

Notes

GOD CALLS HIS PEOPLE ...

THROUGH PRAYER

THROUGH WHAT THEY READ IN THE BIBLE

THROUGH EVENTS

THROUGH SHARED WORSHIP

WHEN WE'RE ON OUR OWN, BEING QUIET

GOD'S CALL

HOW DO I KNOW IF GOD IS CALLING ME? I DON'T WANT TO MISS IT.

In that case you'll know, because you're expecting to hear from him. But there are ways to check.

LIKE WHAT?

Like – does this call match up with the God I know? Does it seem personally meant for me?

IF IT FEELS RIGHT, WHAT SHOULD I DO?

Tell God you are listening and are ready to go where he leads you. Don't go ahead of God, making things happen. Let him lead you.

WHY LISTEN?

WHY REFUSE TO LISTEN?

FOR GOD ALONE MY SOUL IN SILENCE WAITS; TRULY MY HOPE IS IN HIM. HE ALONE IS MY ROCK AND MY SALVATION, MY STRONGHOLD, SO THAT I SHALL NOT BE SHAKEN, IN GOD IS MY SAFETY AND HONOUR; GOD IS MY STRONG ROCK AND MY REFUGE.
— FROM PSALM 62 —

VOCATION (LIKE 'VOCAL') MEANS A CALLING

IT MAY BE A CALLING TO LIFE-LONG WORK

IT MAY BE TO A WAY OF LIFE

IT MAY BE A CALL TO PRAY FOR A PARTICULAR PERSON

IT MAY BE FOR A SHORT-TERM PARTICULAR JOB

YOU MAY BE CALLED TO GET IN TOUCH WITH SOMEONE STRAIGHT AWAY

KEEP YOUR EARS OPEN!

SECOND SUNDAY BEFORE ADVENT

Sunday between 13 and 19 November inclusive

Thought for the day

We are to be on our guard; great anguish will accompany the last days, but all that is good and loving, wise and true will be saved and celebrated for ever.

Readings

Daniel 12:1-3
Psalm 16
Hebrews 10:11-14 (15-18) 19-25
Mark 13:1-8

Aim

To explore how the kingdom of heaven is both in the present and the future.

Starter

Beforehand make a number of inkblot shapes on different pieces of paper, and invite everyone to say what shapes they see in the shapes.

Teaching

In inkblots, clouds and shadows, we can often see pictures. Some people would say that what we see shows our character! Today's readings look into the misty future – to the end of time, and two prophets tell us what they see. One of the prophets is Daniel, and the other is Jesus himself.

First read the passage from Daniel. What pictures does the prophet see? Is it terrifying, hopeful, or a mixture? On a sheet of paper headed 'At that time', write the events in different coloured pens to reflect their mood.

Now look at the Gospel for today, with different people reading the narration and characters involved. Once again, write the events on the sheet in different coloured pens, bearing in mind that today's reading only looks at part of the conversation. Does Jesus seem to be excited about this time, or concerned for his followers? What is it that bothers him? He is wanting to impress on his followers the need to be careful and on our guard, in readiness for these times.

We are left with the sense that it will be a frightening time leading up to the Day of the Lord, with evil multiplying and many being led astray. But there is still the strong certainty that through it all the true followers will be kept safe, and nothing good or loving will be lost. Whatever people are really like will be shown for everyone to see – our motives and secret thoughts, as well as what we choose to let people see normally. It's quite a thought.

Praying

You show me the path of life;
in your presence there is fullness of joy,
and in your right hand are pleasures for evermore.
(From Psalm 16)

Activities

On the sheet they are encouraged to see how the kingdom of heaven is both now and in the future, and there is space for them to try a watercolour painting of the Daniel or the Mark reading.

Discussion starters

1. Are we worried about the right things, or about things which needn't concern us?

2. Do today's readings affect our attitude to evangelism?

Notes

A WATERCOLOUR PAINTING, BASED ON DANIEL 12: 1-3 OR MARK 13: 1-8

THE DAY OF THE LORD

WILL THERE BE AN ACTUAL, REAL DAY WHEN EVERYTHING AS WE KNOW IT COMES TO AN END?

Yes, we are told by the prophets and by Jesus himself. We don't know when or how, but we do know it will happen.

IS THAT WHEN THE KINGDOM OF GOD WILL COME?

Yes and no! Yes, it will come totally when we see Jesus coming in glory as judge and gatherer. But we don't have to wait till then – the kingdom is already here wherever God's will is done and wherever Jesus is allowed to reign.

IN MY LIFE, FOR INSTANCE?

Exactly!

SIGNS OF THE KINGDOM NOW

SIGNS OF THE DAY OF THE LORD TO LOOK FOR

YOU SHOW ME THE PATH OF LIFE;
IN YOUR PRESENCE THERE IS FULLNESS OF JOY,
AND IN YOUR RIGHT HAND ARE PLEASURES FOR EVERMORE.
(-FROM PSALM 16-)

CHRIST THE KING

Sunday between 20 and 26 November inclusive

Thought for the day

Jesus Christ is the everlasting King whose kingdom is not of this world, but grows in the hearts of his people and lasts for ever.

Readings

Daniel 7:9-10, 13-14
Psalm 93
Revelation 1:4b-8
John 18:33-37

Aim

To recognise Jesus Christ as the everlasting King of all.

Starter

Give everyone a large post-it note on which they write ten sentences beginning with 'I am . . .' Then they stick their note to themselves and go round reading one another's statements.

Teaching

It's not easy to decide on ten 'I am . . .' statements, but taken altogether they do give a little idea of who we are. Today, the last Sunday of the Church's year, we are in a way summing up everything we know about Jesus Christ, both on earth and in heaven, and the shorthand for all of that is that he is Christ the King. We'll try to unpack it a bit.

Begin by reading Daniel's vision. It's obviously impossible to describe heaven exactly, but look at the images and talk over what they say to us. Also point out that Daniel was writing long before Jesus had come, yet he 'sees' Jesus entering heaven and being made king.

Now go to the Gospel, reading it with different people taking the different parts. Pilate's job, as Roman governor, is to establish whether this so-called king is likely to pose a threat to the Roman empire. As Jesus says, that would be so if his kingdom were 'of this world'. But it isn't. In what way is the kingdom of heaven not 'of this world'? If the territory of the kingdom of heaven is not geographical, where is it found? (Think back to the parables of the kingdom, and all Jesus' teaching about kingdom living.)

So today we see Jesus at his most weak and vulnerable, humanly speaking, on earth, and entering heaven in glory. All of that is the same Jesus, the Servant King who was obedient even to death on a cross.

Finally look at the reading from Revelation, where Jesus Christ is seen as the faithful witness, the firstborn from the dead, and the ruler of the kings of the earth. We are reminded that Jesus is the visible image of the unseen God, totally faithful to speaking out God's words and revealing his love to us. And one day he will come in glory, seen by everybody.

As we look back over the past year, and all we have learnt of Jesus, it makes us want to worship, and proclaim with Christians all over the world and all through history, that Jesus Christ is Lord!

Praying

Jesus is Lord!
Creation's voice proclaims it,
for by his power each tree and flower
was planned and made.
Jesus is Lord!
The universe declares it;
sun, moon and stars in heaven cry:
Jesus is Lord!

(Taken from the song *Jesus is Lord!* by David J. Mansell
© 1982 Springtide/Word Music (UK)/CopyCare)

Activities

In the activities on the sheet they are helped to hold in balance the power and glory of Jesus' kingship with his humility and obedience – the Servant King. They try to catch hold of the image of heaven as described by Daniel, and look at the idea of the words of the Gloria and God's presence in past, present and future.

Discussion starters

1. How does this faith we celebrate today transform our outlook and enable us to face suffering?

2. What is your vision of heaven?

Notes

NOT OF THIS WORLD

BUT JESUS CAME INTO THIS WORLD, DIDN'T HE? HOW COME HIS KINGDOM IS NOT OF THIS WORLD THEN?

When John writes about 'the world' he isn't thinking of God's wonderful good creation. He means 'worldly', or looking for selfish pleasure and greed.

SO JESUS ISN'T SAYING THE WORLD IS OUTSIDE HIS KINGDOM?

Oh no – God's natural world is part of the kingdom. But Jesus is not a king of a country, like wanting to be another Julius Caesar or something.

WHERE IS HE KING, THEN?

Wherever people love God and love one another. Wherever they invite Jesus to reign.

DRAW IN THE RIGHT BALANCE FOR YOUR CURRENT FAVOURITE CD—

BALANCE

-GRAPHIC EQUALIZER-

VOLUME   0 1 2 3 4 5 6 7 8 9 10 11 12 0

WE HAVE TO GET THE BALANCE RIGHT...

JESUS IS BOTH KING OF GLORY AND POWER ...

... AND THE ONE WHO HUMBLY SERVES OTHERS

WHO WAS

AND IS

AND WILL BE

DANIEL 7: 13-14

JESUS IS LORD!
CREATION'S VOICE PROCLAIMS IT,
FOR BY HIS POWER
EACH TREE AND FLOWER
WAS PLANNED AND MADE.
JESUS IS LORD!
THE UNIVERSE DECLARES IT;
SUN, MOON AND STARS
IN HEAVEN CRY:
JESUS IS LORD!

(Taken from the song *Jesus is Lord!* by David J. Mansell, © 1982 Springtide/ Word Music (UK)/CopyCare)

APPENDIX

Script for First Sunday of Advent

Mark   What's up?

Dawn   Uh? Oh, nothing.

Mark   But there's a Fuse bar here that you haven't eaten.

Dawn   Uh? Oh, so there is.

Mark   And I haven't had any e-mail from you for over a week.

Dawn   Uh? Oh . . . no, I haven't written any.

Mark   Well, what's the matter for heaven's sake?

Dawn   *(sighs)* Well, it's no use.

Mark   What's no use?

Dawn   Everything's no use. Only one person has the key to my freedom and peace of mind, and I'm trapped in this prison.

Mark   Well, ask the person with the key to open it!

Dawn   That's just it – I can't.

Mark   Why ever not?

Dawn   Because I've completely ignored the person with the key for ages, and before that I messed up their life big time. So there's no reason in the world why they should even be friendly ever again – let alone get me out of my mess now.

Mark   You could ask them.

Dawn   No, it's too late for that. I'll just have to recognise that I've blown it for ever.

Mark   Well, you could still ask. Maybe he's super-human in the mercy line. Maybe he still cares for you enough to come and rescue you.

Dawn   Do you think so?

Mark   No harm in trying, is there? After all, he did create you.

Dawn   Yes, that's true. OK. Let's ask him.

Both   O Lord God, I know you've got no reason to hear this prayer after the way we've treated you, but, well, you did make us, remember? Could you find it in your heart to come and rescue us? Sort us out? We need that so badly, and we can't do it ourselves . . .

(A paper dart comes flying in, and they read what is written on it)

Both   'For God so loved the world that he gave his one and only Son, that whoever believes in him shall not perish but have eternal life.'

(They look at one another in excitement, and throw the paper dart up into the air as both shout: YES!)

The Trinity is discussing the Incarnation. Father, Son and Spirit are seated as in the icon of the Holy Trinity. (Sounds of arguments and war.)

The Father What they need is the Spirit of God actually alive in them.

The Spirit That's a very personal thing. How can it be done?

The Son Well, as it's personal, it'll have to be done in person.

The Father That's true.

The Spirit It will mean them meeting the Spirit of God in a human person.

(The Father and the Spirit both look at the Son.)

All three speak together:
That's where you/I come in.

The Son How long for?

The Father It'll happen in stages. First, a year or two in ministry, tied to one time zone and in one area, till they get the hang of it.

The Spirit They won't be able to cope for long with God among them in person.

The Father Exactly. It's bound to end in them expelling you.

The Son You mean killing me?

The Father Sadly, yes. But that opens up a new possibility – stage two.

The Spirit How do you mean?

The Father Our love is stronger than death and cannot be destroyed. Through your risen life the Spirit of God will be available for every person in every place and every time zone.

The Spirit So no one needs to lose out!

The Son They'll be able to live the heaven life while they're alive on earth as well as after death!

The Father That's right!

The Son If I'm going to do a couple of years of Godly ministry as a human, I'll have to do all the growing-up bit as well, won't I?

The Father Oh yes – right from conception; you'll need to be part of the whole human experience.

The Spirit But babies are very vulnerable. Suppose they kill him too early?

The Father It's a risk. It's all a risk.

All But if we don't take it, they'll be thrashing about in the dark for ever. They can't save themselves. They need a Saviour.

Human voices, praying earnestly for help:
O come, O come, Emmanuel, save us and set us free!

The Son It's those faithful watchmen calling again.

All And the time is right. Everything's ready.

The Father Gabriel! Come here a moment, will you. We've got some important messages which need delivering personally . . .

The Servant

The employer is talking on his mobile phone, pacing up and down, with a file open. He's sorting out some complex problem. The office cleaner comes in with feather duster and starts cleaning.

Mr King *(Into phone)* Quite . . . Quite . . . But look at these figures on page 24 . . . *(catches sight of Marg the cleaner)* Marg, get me a strong coffee. And a doughnut or something. *(Returns to phone)* Yes, these figures should have warned us . . . Well, the point is what can we do about it now?

(Marg reappears with coffee and doughnut.)

Marg Coffee, Mr King. It's strong. And a doughnut. *(Puts them on desk)*

Mr King *(Still on phone, listening and making 'mm' noises. Motions with hand for Marg not to interrupt him as he's busy.)* Sorry, Steve, say that again . . . the schedules systematically reduced what? . . . Oh, I see. Yes, of course. So what are you going to do about it?

(Marg continues dusting.)

Mr King *(Still on phone)* Marg, get me the February file – it's there on my desk. *(Talks into phone)* It seems to me we can possibly get ourselves out of this mess, Steve. I've just had an idea.

(Marg brings the February file to Mr King.)

Marg The February file, Mr King.

Mr King *(Takes it without thanking her and starts looking in it. Into phone he says)* Yes, here it is! I'm looking at these figures for the second week of February . . .

(Marg goes back to the dusting. The desk phone rings.)

Mr King Answer that, Marg.

Marg *(Picks up phone)* Hello, Mr King's office. Well, he's very busy at the moment, in an important meeting . . . Oh, I've no idea, I'm only the cleaner here. I just do what I'm told.

The Friends

Norman and Pete walk up to a bench and sit down. They put their rucksacks down.

Pete Phew! That was quite a climb, wasn't it. What a view, though, eh?

Norman Marvellous, isn't it. *(Pause)* Anyway, you were saying about your interview . . .

Pete Oh yeah, that's right. So we've got to decide whether to move or not, basically. And that's a big decision to make.

Norman How does Sheila feel about moving? She settled here, isn't she?

Pete Yes, it would be quite a wrench for her, but you know Sheila, she's willing to give it a go if she feels it's what God wants for us.

Norman Funny, isn't it. This time last year, there you were just made redundant, and no hopes for the future, and now this new door seems to be opening for you. I'm really happy for you, Pete.

Pete Thanks, Norman. Well, you've been a good friend through all this – it's always good to talk things over with you. Shall we be on our way then? *(They get up and walk off.)*

All four characters I no longer call you servants, because a servant doesn't know his master's business. Instead I have called you friends.

Cast your cares
on the Lord.
(Psalm 55:22)

Come unto me all who
labour and are heavy
laden, and I will give
you rest.
(Matthew 11:28)

He will direct your paths.
(Proverbs 3:6)

Small is the gate and
narrow the road that
leads to life.
(Matthew 7:13)

He will not suffer your
foot to be moved.
(Psalm 121:3)

He owns the cattle on a
thousand hills.
(Psalm 50:10)

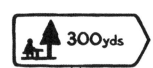

I am the bread of life.
(John 6:35)

Be self-controlled
and alert.
(1 Peter 5:8)

Life's an uphill struggle
without Jesus.